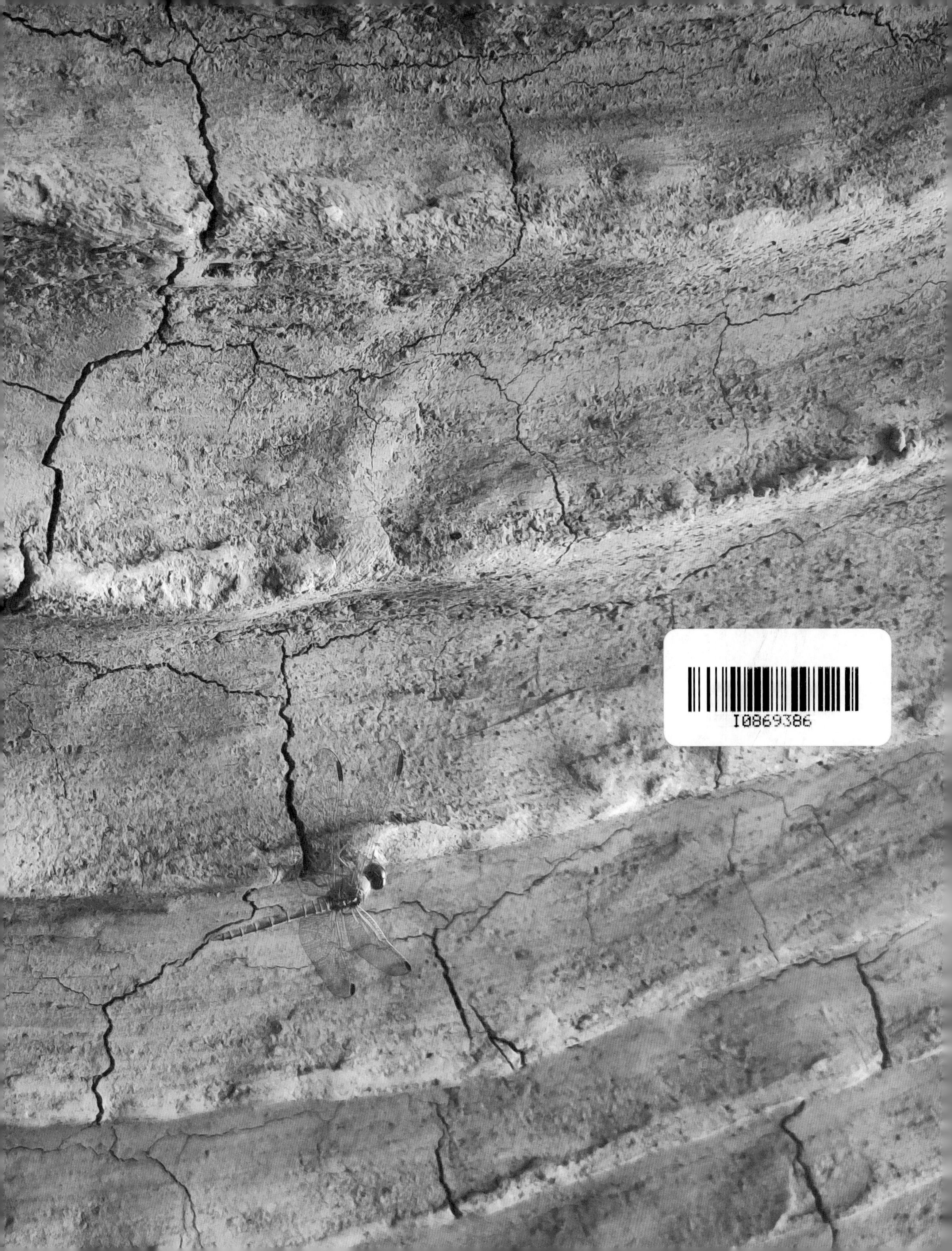

ANNA HERINGER

LIGHT – the Natural Force that Makes Things Visible

LICHT – die natürliche Kraft, die Dinge sichtbar macht

To all the great people who created these wonderful textiles and mud walls.

To nature, which gifts us with the magic of light, which makes beauty visible.

An all die grossartigen Menschen, die diese wunderbaren Textilien und Lehmwände gestaltet haben.

An die Natur, die uns mit der Magie des Lichtes beschenkt, welches Schönheit sichtbar macht.

In den deutschen Texten wird die Schweizer Rechtschreibung verwendet.

ANNA HERINGER

LIGHT

the Natural Force that
Makes Things Visible

die natürliche Kraft,
die Dinge sichtbar macht

LIGHT – the Natural Force that Makes Things Visible

Why a book with a budget that could be used to build a school in Bangladesh? With all my work, I start by asking myself the question "Cui bono?" or, to put it another way: ***"Who should benefit, who should be empowered?"***

In our first conversation, Isabel Zumtobel said that strengthening women is dear to her heart. As an outspoken feminist, this is breaking down open doors for me and I realise who should benefit from this book: ***women in Bangladesh.*** *In the financially disadvantaged, rural north of the country, I work with "Dipdii Textiles", a project in which fair textile art and clothing are produced with the greatest craftsmanship. This initiative empowers women and their families.* ***At the same time, obviously, readers should also gain something*** *because otherwise there is no real need for a book. But what is truly needed in a society that has everything on a material level?*

Contemplating light, *the basic theme of the book, commissioned by the Zumtobel Group, makes me think about light in general, the rays of light in my life and on a global level, in the world community. To be honest, I find the latter difficult.*

LICHT – die natürliche Kraft, die Dinge sichtbar macht

Wozu ein Buch, für dessen Budget man eine Schule in Bangladesch errichten könnte? Bei all meinen Arbeiten stelle ich mir zu Beginn die Frage «Cui bono?» oder anders formuliert: **«Wer soll davon profitieren, wer gestärkt werden?»**

Isabel Zumtobel sagte in unserem ersten Gespräch, dass ihr die Stärkung von Frauen am Herzen liegt. Damit rennt sie bei mir als erklärte Feministin offene Türen ein und mir ist klar, wer von diesem Buch profitieren soll: **Frauen in Bangladesch.** Im finanziell benachteiligten, ländlichen Norden des Landes arbeite ich mit «Dipdii Textiles» zusammen, einem Projekt, in dem faire Textilkunst und Kleidung mit grösstem handwerklichem Können hergestellt werden. Diese Initiative bringt Frauen und ihre Familien in ihre Kraft und Widerstandsfähigkeit. **Gleichzeitig sollen auch die Leser:innen bereichert werden,** denn sonst braucht es nun wirklich kein Buch. Aber was wird wirklich gebraucht in einer Gesellschaft, die auf materieller Ebene alles hat?

Die Kontemplation über Licht, die Grundthematik des Buches, das von der Zumtobel Group beauftragt wurde, lässt mich sinnieren über Licht im Allgemeinen, die Lichtblicke in meinem Leben und auf globaler Ebene, in der Weltgesellschaft. Letztes fällt mir ehrlich gesagt schwer.

Embroidery work, "Dipdii Textiles", Bangladesh /// Stickarbeiten, «Dipdii Textiles», Bangladesch

In a few days' time, the American elections are due, wars are raging and climate change is taking on ever more serious dimensions. Yes, light is needed. In the face of these tragedies, more and more people are falling into a state of heaviness, lethargy and depression. Anxiety is almost becoming the new normal. It is understandable to be afraid of the future, given all the prevailing, conflict-laden chaos. And it is precisely for this reason and at this time that we urgently need to mobilise all our forces to create a good life for the future.

In ein paar Tagen stehen die Wahlen in Amerika an, Kriege toben und der Klimawandel nimmt immer gravierendere Ausmasse an. Ja, Licht braucht es. Immer mehr Menschen fallen angesichts dieser Tragödien in eine Schwere, in eine Lethargie und Depression. Anxiety wird schon fast zum Normalzustand. Zukunftsangst zu haben ist verständlich, bei all dem herrschenden, konfliktschweren Chaos. Und gerade deshalb und jetzt müssen wir dringend alle Kräfte mobilisieren, um ein gutes Leben auch in Zukunft zu schaffen.

I am a stubborn idealist. I don't like to orientate my awareness towards the mere reality. It doesn't give me the strength I need to change things for the better. That's why I focus vehemently on the aspects of my life that I can influence. Sometimes the light at the end of the tunnel seems very, very far away and hardly achievable. But it is there. We have to aim for it, soak it up so that it fills us with energy right up to the brim, and then head for it fearlessly.

Ich bin eine sture Idealistin. An der Realität mag ich mich nicht orientieren. Das gibt mir nicht die nötige Kraft, um Dinge zum Positiven zu verändern. Deshalb fokussiere ich mich vehement auf die Aspekte in meinem Leben, die ich beeinflussen kann. Manchmal erscheint das Licht am Ende des Tunnels sehr, sehr weit weg und kaum erreichbar. Aber es ist da. Man muss es anpeilen, in sich aufsaugen, damit es einem mit Energie füllt bis zum Rand, und dann unerschrocken darauf zusteuern.

Everyone has special talents. And everyone can use these as a lever for change. *And we must not feel intimidated by the scale. The world does not change with one big decision. The world changes with the many small decisions that we make every day and through which we shape our lives. In this book, I want to share a few stories of the levers that have opened up in my life.*

Jede und jeder hat besondere Fähigkeiten. Und jeder kann diese als Hebel für Veränderung einsetzen. Und dabei dürfen wir uns nicht vom Massstab einschüchtern lassen. Die Welt ändert sich nicht mit einer grossen Entscheidung. Die Welt ändert sich mit den vielen kleinen Entscheidungen, die wir alltäglich treffen und mit denen wir unser Leben gestalten. Ein paar Geschichten über die Hebel, die sich in meinem Leben aufgetan haben, und deren Wirkung möchte ich in diesem Buch erzählen.

Under "light", the Oxford Dictionary describes in the first place: "the natural force that makes things visible". *I am lucky that I have been able to get to know many perspectives through my work. As a result, I see many things that would have remained hidden from me if I hadn't stepped out of my European comfort zone.*

Unter «Licht» beschreibt das Oxford Dictionary an erster Stelle: «die natürliche Kraft, die Dinge sichtbar macht.» Ich habe das Glück, dass ich über meine Arbeit viele Perspektiven kennen lernen darf. Dadurch sehe ich so manche Dinge, die mir verborgen geblieben wären, hätte ich mich nicht aus meiner europäischen Komfortzone herausbewegt.

With this book, I shed light on situations, people, challenges and solutions that are often not focussed on enough – that are not "visible" enough. *On the material earth, for example. On the effects of the clothes we wear. On people with disabilities. On the Rohingya refugee crisis. On the imbalance between the masculine and feminine. On the ideal of perfection that makes us sick. In order to heal, as a society and as individuals, this also means really looking at the painful aspects. And they often lose their horror because nothing is purely black or purely white. Rather, it is a variety of colour shades and nuances in which there is a surprising amount of beauty to be discovered if we allow ourselves to do so. Just like the torn, worn fabrics that form the basis of the design of this book.*

Although I am generally referred to as an architect, I am first and foremost an activist. ***In this sense, a part of this book budget and the accompanying exhibition will benefit the project "Dipdii Textiles" in Bangladesh, so that the desire and longing for glimpses of light will be followed by actual positive impact.***

Mit diesem Buch werfe ich gezielt Licht auf Situationen, Menschen, Herausforderungen und Lösungen, die oft zu wenig im Fokus stehen, – die zu wenig «sichtbar» sind. Auf das Material Lehm beispielsweise. Auf die Auswirkungen der Kleidung, die wir tragen. Auf Menschen mit Behinderungen. Auf die Flüchtlingskrise der Rohingya. Auf das Ungleichgewicht zwischen dem Männlichen und Weiblichen. Auf das Ideal von Perfektion, das uns krank macht. Um zu heilen, als Gesellschaft wie als Individuum, bedeutet das auch, wirklich hinzusehen auf die wunden Stellen. Und oft verlieren sie auch an Schrecken, denn nichts ist rein schwarz oder rein weiss. Vielmehr ist es eine Vielfalt an Farbschattierungen und Nuancen, in denen es überraschend viel Schönheit zu entdecken gibt, wenn man sich darauf einlässt. So wie die zerrissenen, abgetragenen Stoffe, welche die Grundlage der Gestaltung dieses Buches darstellen.

Ich werde zwar im Allgemeinen als Architektin bezeichnet, aber in erster Linie bin ich wohl eine Aktivistin. **In diesem Sinne kommt ein Teil dieses Buchbudgets und der begleitenden Ausstellung dem Projekt «Dipdii Textiles» in Bangladesch zugute, auf dass dem Wunsch und Sehnen nach Lichtblicken konkrete positive Wirkung folgt.**

Anna Heringer
October 2024 /// Oktober 2024

Anna Heringer in the caves of the Anandaloy building.
Anna Heringer in den Höhlen des Anandaloy Gebäudes.

Burnt Shirt

Verbrannte Shirt

"Burnt Shirt" (detail), 2012
«Verbranntes Shirt» (Detail), 2012

***In 2012, a strange incident led to this work that I call "Burnt Shirt".** I used it to deal with an attack in which I got involved together with the driver M. Abdul Malek from the NGO Dipshikha.*

We were on the way from Rudrapur, in the north of the country, to the capital Dhaka because my flight was the next day. We were supposed to reach Dhaka around 1 a.m. but heavy fog caused many accidents blocking the roads. It wasn't until around 6 a.m. that we reached the outskirts of Dhaka. I noticed that Malek was becoming more and more nervous. At some point he asked me to sit next to him in the front. When I asked why, he said that cars were no longer allowed to drive after 6 a.m. because the opposition was planning a general strike that banned all vehicles on the streets. Anyone who resisted had to expect violence. I was no stranger to general strikes; my very first day in Bangladesh in 1997 began with a general strike. But I never experienced the level of aggression as particularly high. On the contrary, I always found it very peaceful in the rural north.

Im Jahr 2012 führte eine seltsame Begebenheit zu dieser Arbeit, die ich «Verbranntes Shirt» nenne. Ich habe damit eine Attacke verarbeitet, in die ich gemeinsam mit dem Fahrer M. Abdul Malek von der NGO Dipshikha hineingeriet.

Wir waren auf der Fahrt von Rudrapur, im Norden des Landes, in die Hauptstadt Dhaka, denn mein Flug war für den nächsten Tag geplant. Eigentlich sollten wir Dhaka gegen 1 Uhr nachts erreichen, aber ein heftiger Nebel verursachte viele Unfälle, die die Strassen blockierten. Erst gegen 6 Uhr morgens erreichten wir die Aussengebiete Dhakas. Ich bemerkte, dass Malek immer nervöser wurde. Irgendwann bat er mich, mich neben ihn vorne hinzusetzen. Als ich nach dem Grund fragte, meinte er, dass ab 6 Uhr keine Autos mehr fahren durften, denn es war von der Opposition ein Generalstreik geplant, der jegliche Fahrzeuge auf den Strassen verbot. Wer sich widersetzte, musste mit Gewalt rechnen. Generalstreiks waren mir nicht unbekannt, schon mein allererster Tag in Bangladesch 1997 begann mit einem Generalstreik. Aber ich hatte den Aggressionslevel nie als besonders hoch erlebt. Im Gegenteil, im ländlichen Norden empfand ich es immer als sehr friedlich.

Malek hoffte, dass wir mit einem «Ausländer/Frauen-Faktor» durchkämen, aber plötzlich tauchten aus dem Nebel eine Handvoll Leute auf, die mit einem Baumstamm die Strasse blockierten. Und dann kam eine ganze wütende Menschenmenge auf uns zu. Die ersten Steine trafen die Windschutzscheibe. Malek ging mutig nach draussen, mit dem Versuch, sie zu stoppen. Er wurde sofort zu Boden gerissen, geschlagen und weggezerrt. Ab dem Moment war ich allein im Auto. Die ersten Eisenstangen prallten auf die Windschutzscheibe direkt vor mir ein, die Scheibe begann zu zersplittern und die Hiebe gingen gnadenlos weiter. Ich wusste nicht, ob ich es wagen sollte, mich der wütenden Menge zu stellen oder im Auto zu bleiben. Die Entscheidung fiel innerhalb von Sekunden, ich stürzte aus dem Auto und rannte so schnell ich konnte auf ein paar Buden am Strassenrand zu. Zu meinem grossen Glück widerfuhr mir keine physische Gewalt. Jemand lotste mich in einen Laden. **Als ich mich noch einmal umdrehte, sah ich unser Auto in Flammen.**

Malek was hoping that we would get through with the "foreigner/woman factor", but suddenly a handful of people appeared out of the fog and blocked the road with a tree trunk. And then a whole angry crowd came towards us. The first stones hit the windshield. Malek courageously went outside to try and stop them. He was immediately tackled to the ground, beaten and dragged away. From that moment, on I was alone in the car. The first iron bars hit the windshield directly in front of me, the windows began to shatter and the blows continued mercilessly. I didn't know whether to dare face the angry crowd or stay in the car. The decision was made within seconds, I rushed out of the car and ran as fast as I could towards a few stalls on the side of the road. Luckily for me, I suffered no physical violence. Someone guided me into a store. ***When I turned around, I saw our car in flames.***

I made this shirt with the burn mark months later from textiles that I had transported in the car. Naturally, a lot of thoughts went through my head. ***Something inside me refused to blame the angry people on the streets of Dhaka.*** *The area where the incident occurred is also the area where many textile factories are located. The anger and aggression that build up there definitely correlate with the oppression and exploitation that we all cause: through the clothes we buy. In this moment of realisation, I accepted my responsibility, with the consequence that I would no longer buy these clothes, except as second-hand goods.* ***But above all, this was one of the key moments that led to the founding of "Dipdii Textiles".***

Dieses Shirt mit dem Brandfleck habe ich Monate später aus Textilien, die ich im Auto transportiert hatte, gefertigt. Dabei gingen mir naturgemäss viele Gedanken durch den Kopf. **Etwas in mir weigerte sich, die Schuld auf die wütenden Menschen auf den Strassen Dhakas zu schieben.** Die Gegend, in der jener Vorfall passierte, ist auch die Gegend, in der viele Textilfabriken stehen. Dass sich dort Wut und Aggression aufstauen, hat ganz bestimmt mit der Unterdrückung und Ausbeutung zu tun, die wir alle verursachen: durch die Kleidung, die wir kaufen. In diesem Moment der Realisierung, habe ich dafür meine Verantwortung übernommen, mit der Konsequenz, nicht mehr diese Kleidung zu kaufen, mit Ausnahme als Secondhand-Ware. **Vor allem aber war das einer der Schlüsselmomente, die zur Gründung von «Dipdii Textiles» führten.**

"Burnt Shirt", 2012, sari blankets, partially burnt, 75 × 70 cm
«Verbranntes Shirt», 2012, Sari-Decken, teils verbrannt, 75 × 70 cm

***"Dipdii Textiles" is an initiative for fair textile art and clothing that enables women around the village of Rudrapur to stand on their own two feet economically and to work in an appreciative, friendly atmosphere.** It is a great joy to see how the women have gained strength over the years. So much growth in self-confidence, power and solidarity with one another – and all this with ever-developing creative and craft skills!*

«Dipdii Textiles» ist eine Initiative für faire Textilien, Textilkunst und Kleidung, die es den Frauen rund um das Dorf Rudrapur ermöglicht, wirtschaftlich solide auf eigenen Füssen zu stehen und in einer wertschätzenden, freundschaftlichen Atmosphäre zu arbeiten. Es ist eine grosse Freude zu sehen, wie die Frauen im Lauf der Jahre an Stärke gewinnen. So viel Wachstum an Selbstvertrauen, Kraft und gegenseitiger Solidarität – begleitet von einer stetigen Weiterentwicklung kreativer und handwerklicher Fähigkeiten!

Embroidery is both meditative and community-building. /// Sticken ist sowohl meditativ als auch gemeinschaftsfördernd.

Everyday scenes in Rudrapur, a village in the north of Bangladesh.
Alltagsszenen in Rudrapur, einem Dorf im Norden von Bangladesch.

The majority of Bangladeshis live in rural areas. Rudrapur, which stands for many villages in Bangladesh, shows how people are able to build their habitat with their own resources: using their hands, local mud and bamboo. People produce food and many daily goods themselves. The neighbourhoods have developed over generations and social networks are strong.

Women feel safe in public places, children enjoy their village as a fantastic playground. Elderly people find places to keep watch over a goat under a tree. ***As a result, the village has a high degree of quality of life and resilience.***

Die Mehrheit der Menschen in Bangladesch lebt in ländlichen Gebieten. Rudrapur (das für viele Dörfer in Bangladesch steht) zeigt, wie Menschen ihren Lebensraum aus eigenen Mitteln aufbauen können: mit ihren Händen, lokalem Lehm und Bambus. Die Menschen produzieren Lebensmittel und viele Güter des täglichen Bedarfs selbst. Die Siedlungen haben sich über Generationen hinweg entwickelt und die sozialen Netzwerke sind stark.

Frauen fühlen sich im öffentlichen Raum sicher, Kinder geniessen ihr Dorf als tollen Spielplatz. Ältere Menschen finden Orte, an denen sie unter einem Baum auf eine Ziege aufpassen und sich unterhalten können. **Dadurch verfügt das Dorf über ein hohes Mass an Lebensqualität und Widerstandsfähigkeit.**

Every piece of clothing has a spatial correspondence.
And this place can be an inhumane place or a good one.

Jedes Kleidungsstück hat eine räumliche Entsprechung.
Und dieser Ort kann ein unmenschlicher oder ein guter sein.

"Dipdii Textiles" embroidery masters working on the tapestry "One Planet – One Family". Embroidery on sari blanket, embroidery on silk. /// Stickmeisterinnen von «Dipdii Textiles» bei der Arbeit an dem Wandteppich «One Planet – One Family». Stickerei auf Sari-Decke, Stickerei auf Seide.

Homework is done in the extended living room, the village street. /// Hausaufgaben werden im erweiterten Wohnzimmer, der Dorfstrasse, erledigt.

রুদ্রপুর
rudrapur
1 METI-School (05/06)
2 DESI-building (07/08)
3 Family houses (07/08)
4 Anandaloy building
Existing buildings
Bamboo forest
raw material source
Ponds
raw material source for clay
Area above field-level
Paddy fields
Dipshikha campus

The village Rudrapur is an example of a lifestyle rooted in self-sufficiency. *The ponds serve not only the purpose of fish cultivation – they are also the excavation source for the mud to build the homes. The bamboo for the roof construction is planted around the hamlets. Food grows all around the village. With the production of the most essential materials within close vicinity, the level of resilience is very high.*

"Village map of Rudrapur" and "Map caption", 2017, embroidery on sari blankets, 195 × 138 cm / 96 × 108 cm
«Dorfplan von Rudrapur» und «Kartenlegende», 2017, Stickerei auf Sari-Decken, 195 × 138 cm / 96 × 108 cm

Das Dorf Rudrapur ist ein Beispiel für einen Lebensstil, der auf Selbstversorgung basiert. Die Teiche dienen nicht nur der Fischzucht, sie dienen auch als Aushub-Quelle für den Lehm zum Bau der Häuser. Der Bambus für die Dachkonstruktion wird rund um die Weiler gepflanzt. Lebensmittel wachsen überall in und um das Dorf herum. Da die wichtigsten Materialien in unmittelbarer Nähe produziert werden, ist der Grad an Resilienz sehr hoch.

However, because of the growing population, land resources are becoming scarce and are no longer sufficient to sustain a family through agriculture alone. ***There is a lack of jobs and this leads people to leave their villages. To me, the project "Dipdii Textiles" is primarily an exemplary action against the rural-to-urban migration in order to keep the level of autonomy high.***

The production of fast fashion has a massive influence on people's lives. *From all around the country, people move to the urban textile production hubs. They leave their own homes in the villages to stay in rented rooms. Childcare is a big problem. They pay for water, for sanitation, for transportation. Women don't feel safe in public areas.*

Aufgrund der wachsenden Bevölkerung werden die Bodenressourcen knapp und reichen nicht mehr aus, um eine Familie allein durch Landwirtschaft zu erhalten. **Es gibt einen Mangel an Arbeitsplätzen und dies führt dazu, dass die Menschen ihre Dörfer verlassen. Für mich ist das Projekt «Dipdii Textiles» in erster Linie eine exemplarische Massnahme gegen die Landflucht, um die Selbständigkeit hochzuhalten.**

Die Produktion von Fast Fashion hat einen massiven Einfluss auf das Leben der Menschen. Aus dem ganzen Land ziehen Menschen in die städtischen Textilproduktionszentren. Sie verlassen ihre eigenen Häuser in den Dörfern, um in gemieteten Zimmern zu leben. Kinderbetreuung ist ein grosses Problem. Sie zahlen für Wasser, für sanitäre Einrichtungen, für Transport. Frauen fühlen sich in öffentlichen Räumen nicht sicher.

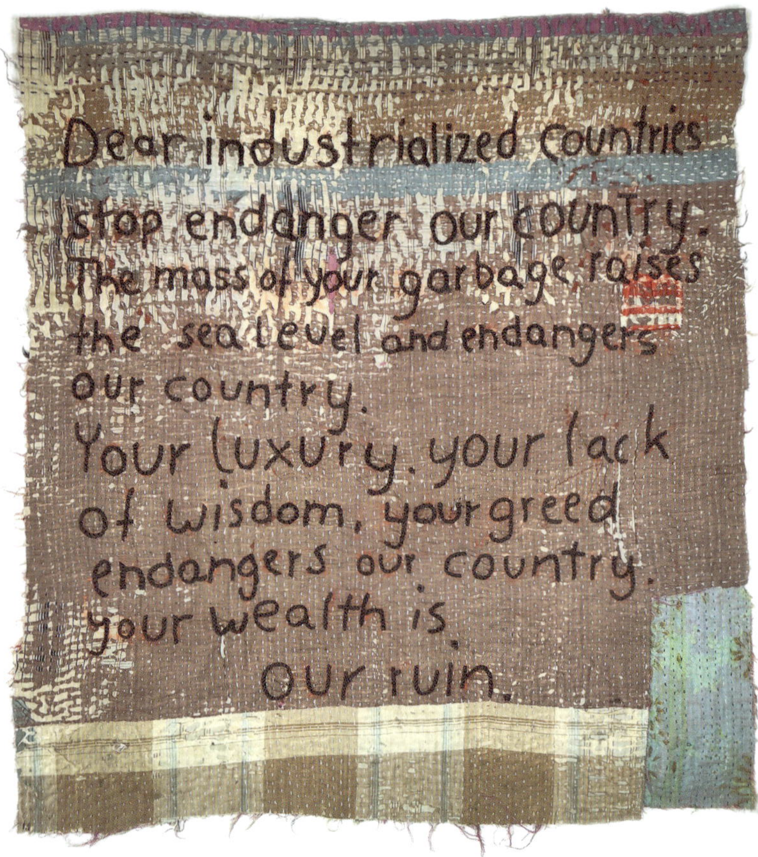

"Letters to Europe". This contemplation on fast fashion was created in collaboration with students from Austria, Germany and former factory workers in Bangladesh, 2020–2023. /// «Briefe an Europa». Diese Kontemplationen über Fast Fashion sind in Zusammenarbeit mit Schüler:innen aus Österreich, Deutschland und mit den ehemaligen Fabrikarbeiterinnen in Bangladesch entstanden, 2020–2023.

He watches the sun passing by turning into red going to rest under blankets of rising water
There will be a day, when we'll have to leave. 'cause our land will be no more.
Our lives will never be the same, once the flood comes rushing in.
Money is the key to happiness. But is it really?
My life is full of colours But soon there will only be grey tones
There will be no laughter, no colours
in the sun's
light
future
I have one question. How does clean air smell like?
I am afraid of tomorrow
darkness.
destroy

There is another way. An alternative without the exploitation caused by mass-produced clothes. *"Dipdii Textiles" is designed for a decentralised production in the village, where the quality of life and space are humane and beautiful.*

At the beginning of the "Dipdii Textiles" project, there was no building. As a mother of a young child myself, I thought it would be best if the women were given a piece of fabric and the design so that they could work on the embroidery at home and at their own pace.

But I hadn't taken one thing into account: ***in Bangladesh, embroidery is traditionally an activity that is usually done in a group of women, where people bond by doing things together and talking.*** *The women had a great need to meet up and exchange emotions while they were working on their crafts. About their worries and needs, but also about the joys of everyday life. Women rarely go to the "tea stall" to chat; that's usually only done by men. The "Dipdiis" wanted social interaction and a place for that.*

Es gibt einen anderen Weg. Eine Alternative ohne die Ausbeutung, die durch Massenproduktion entsteht. «Dipdii Textiles» ist für eine dezentrale Produktion im Dorf konzipiert, wo die Lebensqualität und der Raum menschenwürdig und schön sind.

Zu Beginn des Projektes «Dipdii Textiles» gab es kein Gebäude. Selbst Mutter eines kleinen Kindes, dachte ich damals, es sei das Beste, die Frauen bekämen ein Stück Stoff und das Design ausgehändigt, so dass sie die Stickerei zuhause und zeitlich flexibel bearbeiten können.

Aber ich hatte eines nicht berücksichtigt: **Stickarbeit ist traditionell in Bangladesch eine Tätigkeit, die meist in einer Runde von Frauen gemacht wird, wo das gemeinsame Tun und Reden verbindet.** Die Frauen hatten ein grosses Bedürfnis, sich zu treffen und sich während des handwerklichen Schaffens, emotional auszutauschen. Über die Sorgen und Nöte, aber auch über die Freuden des Alltäglichen. Frauen gehen selten zum Ratschen in den «tea stall», die Teestube, das machen meist nur die Männer. Aber den sozialen Austausch, den brauchte es für die «Dipdiis» und den Raum dazu.

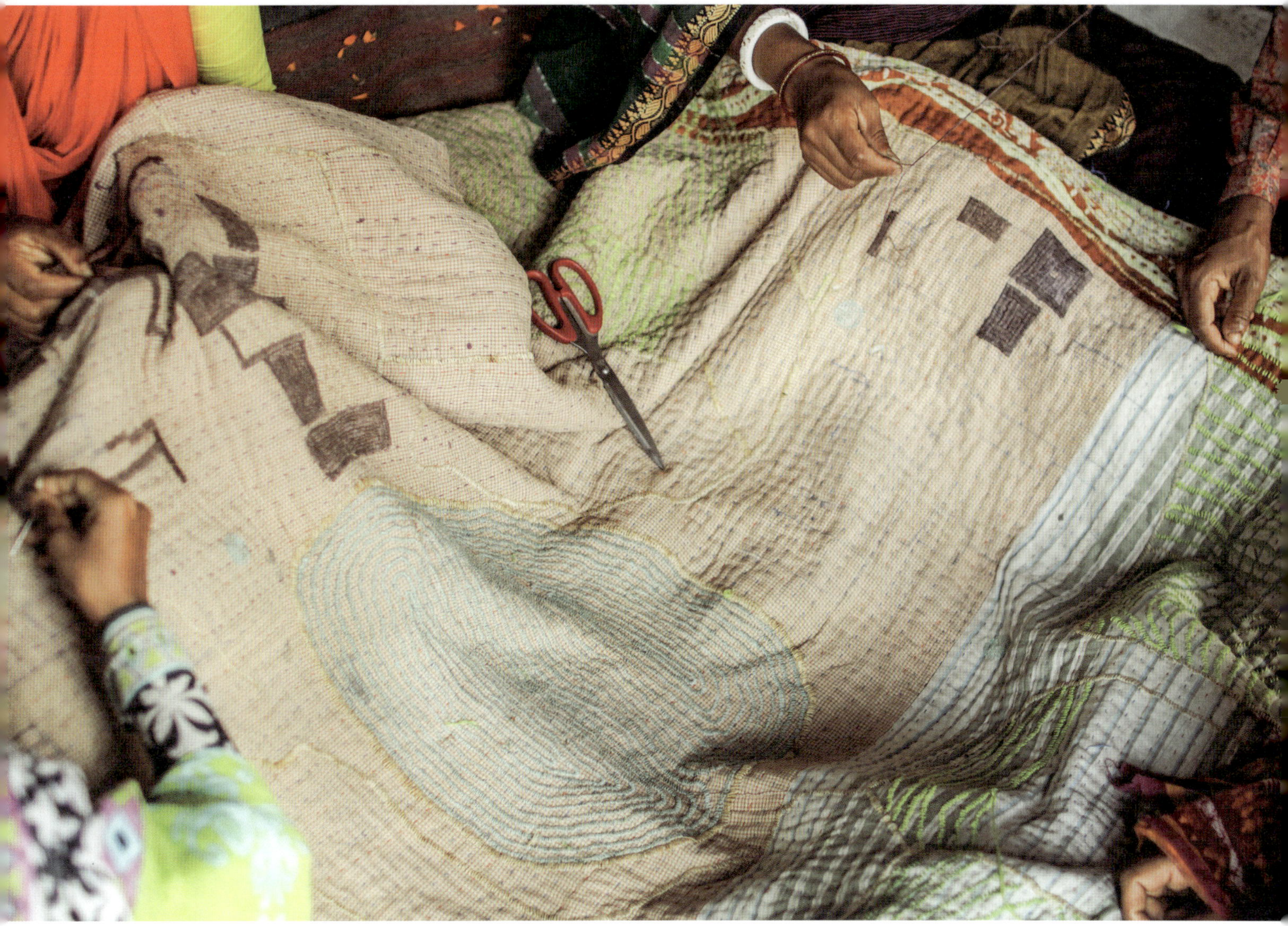

About five women work together for several months on an embroidered wall hanging.
An einem bestickten Wandbehang arbeiten etwa fünf Frauen mehrere Monate.

The Anandaloy building is used as a textile workshop and as a therapy centre for people with disabilities. It was built in 2020 by local craftspeople using earth, bamboo and straw. /// Das Anandaloy Gebäude wird genutzt als Textilwerkstatt und als Therapiestätte für Menschen mit Behinderung. Es wurde 2020 von lokalen Handwerker:innen aus Lehm, Bambus und Stroh gebaut.

Anandaloy: Centre for People with Disabilities and "Dipdii Textiles" Workshop, Rudrapur, Bangladesh, 2020
Anandaloy: Zentrum für Menschen mit Behinderung und «Dipdii Textiles»-Studio, Rudrapur, Bangladesch, 2020

When a new centre for people with disabilities was being built, I planned an additional space for the embroiderers and seamstresses. That's how the Anandaloy Centre came about. "Anandaloy" means "place of unbridled joy" in English.

Beim Bau eines neuen Zentrums für Menschen mit Behinderung plante ich daher einen Raum für die Stickerinnen und Schneiderinnen mit. So entstand das Anandaloy Zentrum. «Anandaloy» bedeutet auf Deutsch «Ort der unbändigen Freude».

Anandalay
Ananda loke
mongolo loke
Biroja sotta sundoro.
Rabindrnat
Tagore

tailoring
work shop

28/29: "Elevation of the Anandaloy building", 2024, embroidery on sari blanket, 210 × 165 cm
28/29: «Ansicht des Anandaloy Gebäudes», 2024, Stickerei auf Sari-Decke, 210 × 165 cm

30: "Anandaloy building: upper floor plan" (detail), 2019, embroidery on sari blanket, 160 × 120 cm
30: «Anandaloy Gebäude: Grundriss Obergeschoss» (Detail), 2019, Stickerei auf Sari-Decke, 160 × 120 cm

31: "Anandaloy building: ground floor plan", 2019, embroidery on sari blanket, 190 × 120 cm
31: «Anandaloy Gebäude: Grundriss Erdgeschoss», 2019, Stickerei auf Sari-Decke, 190 × 120 cm

These embroideries are based on drawings by children who portrayed themselves in front of their therapy centre. 2024, 81 × 75 cm and 63 × 59 cm (Project management: Klara Haug)
Grundlage für diese Stickereien sind Zeichnungen von Kindern, die sich selbst vor ihrem Therapiezentrum porträtiert haben. 2024, 81 × 75 cm und 63 × 59 cm (Projektmanagement: Klara Haug)

Meet the artists (pages 32–35):
Die Künstler:innen (Seiten 32–35):
Matura, Manosi Rani, Anupam, Tajniza, Eti Rani

The ground floor of the Anandaloy building is used for various forms of therapy. We asked the users to draw themselves with the building. ***These are their portraits. And their superpowers! All of them transformed into embroideries – on the first floor of the building.***

Das Erdgeschoss des Anandaloy Gebäudes wird für verschiedene Therapieformen genutzt. Wir haben die Nutzer gebeten, sich selbst mit dem Gebäude zu zeichnen. **Dies sind ihre Porträts. Und ihre Superkräfte! Sie wurden alle in Stickereien umgesetzt – im ersten Stock des Gebäudes.**

The children with special needs – and special superpowers – show their drawings. /// Die Kinder mit besonderen Bedürfnissen – und besonderen Superkräften – zeigen ihre Zeichnungen.

My Superpower

Meine Superkraft

People with disabilities are far too often overlooked. ***But there is so much joy, liveliness and beauty to discover because of them ...!***

Menschen mit Behinderungen werden viel zu oft übersehen. **Dabei gibt es gerade mit ihnen so viel Freude, Lebendigkeit und Schönheit zu entdecken ...!**

These are the drawing responses of children with special needs to the question: "What is your superpower?" The drawings were transformed into embroideries by "Dipdii Textiles". (Project management: Klara Haug) /// Das sind die zeichnerischen Antworten der Kinder mit speziellen Bedürfnissen auf die Frage: «Was ist deine Superkraft?» Die Zeichnungen wurden von «Dipdii Textiles» in Stickereien umgesetzt. (Projektmanagement: Klara Haug)

Anandalay
আনন্দালয়
Ananda loke
mongola loke
birajo sotto sundoro
Rabindranath Tagore
Centre for people with disabilities
&
Dipdii Textiles
Workshop
Rudrapur 2019

We design spaces not only as architects and planners but above all as consumers.

Wir gestalten Räume nicht nur als Architekt:innen und Planer:innen, sondern v. a. auch als Konsument:innen.

36–38: Interior of the "Dipdii Textiles" studio with a wall hanging showing the embroidered floor plan of the building. 2022
36–38: Innenraum des «Dipdii Textiles» Ateliers mit einem Wandbehang, der den gestickten Grundriss des Gebäudes zeigt. 2022

39: The veranda on the upper floor of the Anandaloy building, made of clay and bamboo. /// 39: Die Veranda im Obergeschoss des Anandaloy Gebäudes, gebaut aus Lehm und Bambus.

Patches

Flicken

"Karma", upcycled sari blanket, 221 × 171 cm
«Karma», upgecycelte Sari-Decke, 221 × 171 cm

*"Clouds come floating into my life,
no longer to carry rain or usher storm,
but to add colour to my sunset sky."*

Rabindranath Tagore

«Wolken ziehen in mein Leben, nicht länger um Regen zu bringen oder Sturm heraufzubeschwören, sondern um meinem Sonnenuntergangshimmel Farbe zu verleihen.»

Rabindranath Tagore

42–43: "Holi" (Festival of Colours), upcycled sari blanket, 210 × 153 cm
42–34: «Holi» (Fest der Farben), upgecycelte Sari-Decke, 210 × 153 cm

44–45: "Suryasta" (Sunset), upcycled sari blanket, 170 × 214 cm
44–45: «Suryasta» (Sonnenuntergang), upgecycelte Sari-Decke, 170 × 214 cm

That's exactly how I feel when I look at the torn, mended sari blankets – it's the injuries, the repaired areas that make these textiles so beautiful and unique.

These textiles consist of several layers of saris and lungis or dhotis and originate from the village of Rudrapur in the north of Bangladesh. Traditionally, women there are given a new sari, the traditional 8-meter-long wrap-around dress, for Durga Puja, an important Hindu festival, or for Eid, the main Muslim festival. The men dress in new lungis or dhotis, both of which are wrap-around skirts.

Genauso fühle ich, wenn ich die zerrissenen, geflickten Sari-Decken betrachte, es sind die Verletzungen, die reparierten Stellen, welche diese Textilien so schön und einzigartig machen.

Diese Textilien bestehen aus mehreren Schichten Saris und Lungis oder Dhotis und stammen aus dem Dorf Rudrapur im Norden von Bangladesch. Traditionell bekommen dort die Frauen zur Durga Puja, einem wichtigen Hindufest oder zu Eid, dem Hauptfest der Muslime, einen neuen Sari, das in etwa acht Meter lange traditionelle Wickelkleid. Die Männer kleiden sich in neue Lungis oder Dhotis ein, beides sind Wickelröcke.

"Suryodaya" (Sunrise), upcycled sari blanket, 158 × 191 cm /// «Suryodaya» (Sonnenaufgang), upgecycelte Sari-Decke, 158 × 191 cm

The saris and the men's skirts are woven from fine cotton fabric. ***When they are worn out or torn, they are not thrown away but made into blankets with countless small hand stitches in several layers of fabric.*** *Several women from the neighbourhood come together and joke and laugh while embroidering.*

Die Saris und die Wickelröcke der Männer sind aus feinem Baumwollstoff gewebt. **Sind diese abgetragen oder eingerissen, werden sie nicht entsorgt, sondern mit unzähligen kleinen Handstichen in mehreren Stofflagen zu Decken gefertigt.** Dazu kommen mehrere Frauen aus der Nachbarschaft zusammen und es wird gescherzt und gelacht während man stickt.

Detail of "Gaye holud" (Pre-wedding ceremony during which the bride and groom are given a rubbing with turmeric paste), upcycled sari blanket, 177 × 87 cm
Detail von «Gaye Holud» (Feier am Tag vor der Hochzeit, bei der die Brautleute mit Kurkuma Paste eingerieben werden), upgecycelte Sari-Decke, 177 × 87 cm

In the hot months, the blanket becomes a sheet that is placed over the simple sleeping mattresses, as the surface of the blankets is nice and soft. The whole family often sleeps in one bed. During the nights, we process everyday life, the past days and years in our sleep, tossing and turning, and ***the different layers of fabric reappear, each representative of a certain period in our lives.***

In den heissen Monaten wird die Decke zum Leintuch, das über die einfachen Schlafmatratzen gelegt wird, denn die Oberfläche der Decken ist schön weich. Oft schläft die ganze Familie in einem Bett. In den Nächten verarbeiten wir den Alltag, die vergangenen Tage und Jahre im Schlaf, wälzen hin und her und **dabei kommen die unterschiedlichen Stoffschichten wieder zum Vorschein, die alle repräsentativ für eine bestimmte Zeitspanne im Leben stehen.**

51: "Dhan matti" (Paddy field), upcycled sari blanket, 120 × 180 cm
51: «Dhan matti» (Reisfeld), upgecycelte Sari-Decke, 120 × 180 cm

52: "Bagan" (Garden), upcycled sari blanket, 95 × 218 cm
52: «Bagan» (Garten), upgecycelte Sari-Decke, 95 × 218 cm

53: "Barsakala" (Rainy season), upcycled sari blanket, 110 × 187 cm
53: «Barsakala» (Regenzeit), upgecycelte Sari-Decke, 110 × 187 cm

54/55: "Nil bari" (Blue house), upcycled sari blanket, 172 × 146 cm
54/55: «Nil bari» (Blaues Haus), upgecycelte Sari-Decke, 172 × 146 cm

"Ghost", upcycled sari blanket, 150 × 230 cm
«Ghost», upgecycelte Sari-Decke, 150 × 230 cm

"This yellow one here, I wore it when we went to my sister-in-law's house on the bicycle rickshaw. It got caught in the wheels back then …"

«Dieser Gelbe hier, den hatte ich an, als wir mit der Fahrradrikscha zur Schwägerin fuhren. Der ist mir damals in die Räder kommen …»

“The pink sari in this layer, I wore it when I was pregnant with my daughter ...”
«Der rosa Sari in dieser Schicht, den habe ich getragen, als ich mit meiner Tochter schwanger war ...»
“... and this was the lungi my husband was wearing when the water buffalo stepped on his foot, ah, that was a difficult year ...”
«... und das war der Lungi, den mein Mann trug, als ihm der Wasserbüffel auf den Fuss gestiegen ist, ah, das war ein mühsames Jahr ...»
“This patched hole here, my husband burned it with a cigarette, that almost caused a fire. How often have I told him to quit smoking!”
«Das geflickte Loch hier hat mein Mann mit einer Zigarette reingebrannt, beinahe hätte es einen grossen Brand gegeben. Ich hab’s ihm ja immer gesagt, er soll aufhören zu rauchen!»

58/59: Detail of the back of "Karma", upcycled sari blanket, 221 × 171 cm
58/59: Detail von der Rückseite von «Karma», upgecycelte Sari-Decke, 221 × 171 cm

60/61: Detail of "Suryodaya" (Sunrise), upcycled sari blanket, 158 × 191 cm
60/61: Detail von «Suryodaya» (Sonnenaufgang), upgecycelte Sari-Decke, 158 × 191 cm

These and similar stories
are interwoven in these blankets.

Diese und ähnliche Geschichten sind in diesen Decken verwoben.

Earth and Light

Erde und Licht

Earthen sculpture for the Venice Biennale, designed by Heringer & Rauch, 2016
Lehmskulptur für die Biennale in Venedig, entworfen von Heringer & Rauch, 2016

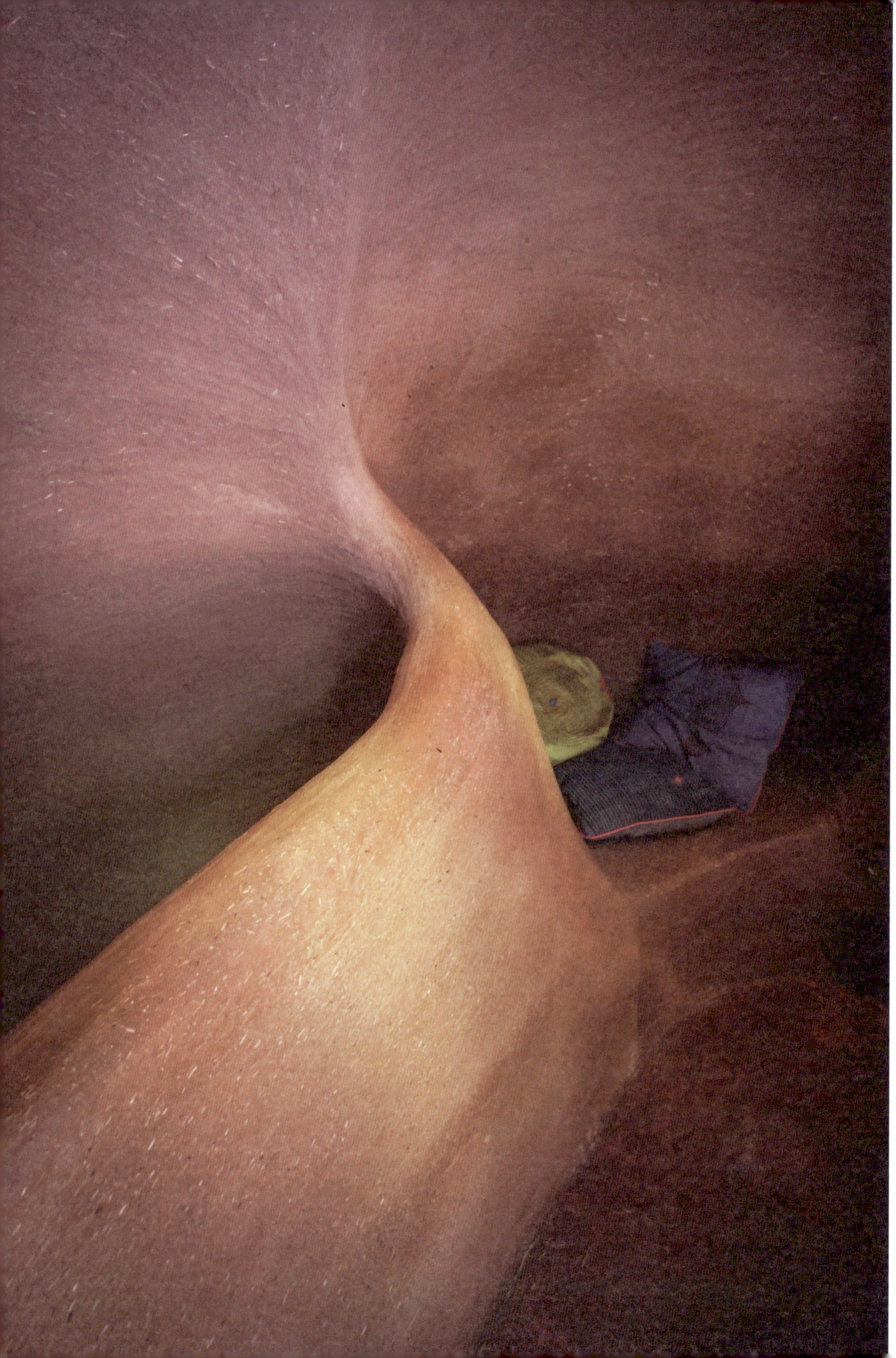

There is an inherent magic in the connection between light and earth. *This is also reflected in the way light – whether natural or artificial – touches the clay surfaces, which always appear spherical and soft, almost caressing. It never has a hardness, probably also because the surfaces are not perfect and are created by hand.*

Der Verbindung von Licht und Erde wohnt ein magischer Zauber inne. Das zeigt sich auch darin, dass Licht – egal ob natürlich oder Kunstlicht – auf Lehmoberflächen treffend, immer sphärisch und weich, fast liebevoll anmutet. Nie hat es eine Härte, vermutlich auch, weil die Oberflächen nicht perfekt und von Händen geschaffen sind.

Interior of the "Monolith" sculpture, designed by Heringer & Rauch for OMICRON electronics in Klaus, Austria /// Innenansicht der Skulptur «Monolith», entworfen von Heringer & Rauch für OMICRON electronics in Klaus, Österreich.

The clay sculpture is a contemplative relaxing space for employees. /// Die Lehmskulptur ist ein kontemplativer Entspannungsort für Mitarbeiter:innen.

At the headquarters of OMICRON electronics in Vorarlberg, Austria, the atrium is illuminated by the "Zeppelin", a hanging wooden construction, partially plastered with clay and covered with textile. ***Here, three of my favourite elements come together: earth, light and textile, with the textile – for me – manifesting the light.*** *The textile used is raw, non-violent silk from "Little Flower India", an association to support students who grew up in a leprosy village in Bihar, India.*

In Vorarlberg, Österreich, im Hauptsitz von OMICRON electronics wird das Atrium erhellt durch den «Zeppelin», eine hängende Holzkonstruktion, die teils mit Lehm verputzt und mit Textil bespannt ist. **Hier kommen drei meiner Lieblingselemente zusammen: Lehm, Licht und Textil, wobei das Textil für mich das Licht manifestiert.** Der verwendete Stoff ist rohe, gewaltfreie Seide von «Little Flower India», einem Verein zur Unterstützung von Student:innen, die in einem Lepradorf in Bihar, Indien, aufgewachsen sind.

66: The sculptures "Monolith" and "Zeppelin" offer different atmospheres for relaxation and exchange in an atrium at the headquarters of OMICRON electronics. 66: Die Skulpturen «Monolith» und «Zeppelin» bieten unterschiedliche Atmosphären zum Entspannen und Austauschen in einem Atrium im Hauptsitz von OMICRON electronics.

67: Interior of the Zeppelin, a wooden structure, clad with red clay plaster and non-violent silk from the NGO "Little Flower India". /// 67: Innenansicht des Zeppelins, einer Holzkonstruktion, verkleidet mit rotem Lehmputz und gewaltfreier Seide der NGO «Little Flower India».

Daylight takes on a major role in my creative work as an architect. *The colours look different in every place. The golden light in Bangladesh makes the pink at the METI School really crisp. In combination with textiles, it brings a wonderful softness to the interiors. It is most beautiful when the wind blows gently into the semi-transparent textiles, then the light is experienced even more vividly.*

Tageslicht nimmt in meinem kreativen Schaffen als Architektin eine grosse Rolle ein. Die Farben wirken an jedem Ort anders. Das goldene Licht in Bangladesch macht das Pink bei der METI-Schule so richtig knackig. In Verbindung mit Textilien kommt es mit einer wunderbaren Weichheit in die Innenräume. Am schönsten ist es, wenn der Wind sanft in die semitransparenten Textilien bläst, dann wird das Licht noch lebendiger wahrgenommen.

68/69: METI School, Bangladesh. The translucent, coloured sari textiles create a poetic atmosphere in the classrooms on the ground floor.
68/69: METI-Schule, Bangladesch. Die durchscheinenden, farbigen Sari-Textilien schaffen eine poetische Atmosphäre in den Klassenräumen im Erdgeschoss.

70/71: East façade of METI School, Rudrapur, Bangladesh, made of mud and bamboo. /// 70/71: Ostfassade der METI-Schule, Rudrapur, Bangladesch, aus Lehm und Bambus.

Archaic spaces such as the caves in the METI School also need some darkness – along with accentuated light falls.

Archaische Räume wie die Höhlen in der METI-Schule brauchen auch etwas Dunkelheit – zusammen mit akzentuierten Lichteinfällen.

72/73: "Joyful learning" is the school's motto. Cave-like rooms were by far the favourite rooms of my childhood – and I think these archaic typologies work just as well in Bavaria as they do in Bangladesh. That's why they were integrated into the back wall of the classroom. /// 72/73: «Freude am Lernen» ist das Motto der Schule. Höhlenartige Räume waren mit Abstand die Lieblingsräume meiner Kindheit – und ich denke, diese Grundschultypologie funktioniert in Bayern genauso gut wie in Bangladesch. Deshalb wurden Höhlen in die Rückwand des Klassenzimmers integriert.

74/75: The Anandaloy building also has caves underneath the ramp, which are part of the therapy offered in that building. /// 74/75: Auch das Anandaloy Gebäude verfügt über Höhlen unter der Rampe, die Teil der in diesem Gebäude angebotenen Therapie sind.

The search for the new super material, green concrete, is in full swing in the construction industry ... Yet, nature has provided a super material since time immemorial and it is available everywhere: under our feet. ***Earth, clay is the champion when it comes to regenerative, ecological construction.***

It is the only material that can be used for load-bearing walls, floors, plastering and, in combination with wood, ceilings without any additional additives and that can be recycled as often as required without any loss of quality. When it is no longer needed, it becomes a garden again. ***From carbon-neutral and regenerative structures to socially just processes, it is the most important building material we have on this planet tackling both growing social injustice and climate change. Bonus on top of it: Mud is beautiful. And when light meets earth, it is magical.***

Die Suche nach dem neuen Supermaterial, dem grünen Beton, läuft in der Baubranche auf vollen Touren ... Dabei hat die Natur ein Supermaterial seit Urzeiten bereitgestellt und es ist überall vorhanden: zu unseren Füssen. **Erde, Lehm ist der Champion, wenn es um regeneratives, ökologisches Bauen geht.**

Es ist das einzige Material, das man ohne weitere Zuschläge für tragende Wände, Böden, Verputze, und in Kombination mit Holz für Decken verwenden kann, das beliebig oft recycelbar ist und das ohne Qualitätsverlust. Wird es nicht mehr gebraucht, wird es wieder zum Garten. **Von CO_2-neutralen und regenerativen Konstruktionen bis hin zu sozial gerechten Prozessen ist es das wichtigste Baumaterial, das wir auf diesem Planeten haben, um sowohl die wachsende soziale Ungerechtigkeit als auch den Klimawandel zu bekämpfen. Ein Bonus obendrein: Lehm ist wunderschön. Und wenn Licht auf Erde trifft, ist es magisch.**

Rammed earth has an especially beautiful surface: it is both raw and archaic as well as warm and emotional.
Stampflehm hat eine besonders schöne Oberfläche: Er ist sowohl schlicht und archaisch als auch warm und emotional.

The site of METI School was completely low-tech. But earthen walls can be constructed both in low-tech and high-tech modes of construction, which makes earth construction an applicable strategy for sustainability worldwide, in any context.
Der Standort der METI-Schule war komplett low-tech. Lehmmauern können jedoch sowohl in Low- als auch in High-Tech-Bauweisen errichtet werden, was sie zu einer global einsetzbaren, kontextunabhängigen Lösung für nachhaltiges Bauen macht.

"We know more about the movement of celestial bodies than about the soil underfoot." Leonardo da Vinci

«Wir wissen mehr über die Bewegung der Himmelskörper als über den Boden unter unseren Füssen.» Leonardo da Vinci

In the DESI building, the bamboo weaving of the verandas characterises the building with its ornamental shadows. Dried leaves between a translucent ceiling and spanned sari fabrics transform the veranda into a nuanced symphony of light, shadows and colours.

Beim DESI Gebäude prägt das Bambus Geflecht der Veranden mit seinem ornamentalem Schattenwurf das Gebäude. Getrocknete Blätter zwischen einer transluzenten Decke und gespannten Sari-Stoffen verwandeln die Veranda in eine nuancierte Symphonie aus Licht, Schattenspielen und Farben.

78/79: One of the most pleasant lighting situations is patched light, a spectrum of shades we also find when walking in the forest. At the DESI Vocational Training Centre in Rudrapur, this situation has been created by dried leaves under a transparent roof, which have been enchanted with colours through the use of saris. /// 78/79: Eine der angenehmsten Beleuchtungssituationen ist geflecktes Licht, ein Spektrum von Schattierungen, das wir auch bei einem Waldspaziergang finden. Im DESI Berufsausbildungszentrum in Rudrapur wurde diese Situation durch getrocknete Blätter unter einem transparenten Dach geschaffen, die durch die Verwendung von Saris mit Farben verzaubert wurden.

80/81: First Floor of METI School, Rudrapur, Bangladesh
80/81: Obergeschoss der METI-Schule, Rudrapur, Bangladesch

In Ghana, I deliberately design with projections and recesses on the outer wall to give rhythm to the façade through the resulting shadow play. Originally planned in orthogonal shape, the hands of the plastering women intuitively shaped the window openings roundish. That's true co-creation!

In Ghana gestalte ich ganz bewusst mit Vor- und Rücksprüngen an der Aussenwand, um durch das daraus resultierende Schattenspiel der Fassade Rhythmik zu verleihen. Ursprünglich in orthogonaler Form geplant, wurden die Fensteröffnungen von den Händen der Verputzerinnen intuitiv rundlich gestaltet. Das ist wahre Co-Kreation!

82/83: Preparation of rammed earth floor at the Don Bosco Earth Campus in Ghana. /// 82/83: Vorbereitung des Stampflehmbodens im Don Bosco Earth Campus in Ghana.

84–87: The openings of the classrooms of the Don Bosco Earth Campus in Ghana follow a playful rhythmicity.
84–87: Die Öffnungen der Klassenräume des Don Bosco Earth Campus in Ghana folgen einer spielerischen Rhythmik.

88/89: Building site in Ghana. In the traditional Atakpamé technique, the moist clay is applied in layers by hand.
88/89: Baustelle in Ghana. Bei der traditionellen Atakpamé Technik wird der feuchte Lehm schichtweise per Hand aufgetragen.

The same principle of shadow play is applied on a smaller scale, in the intuitively and participatorily designed reliefs of clay plaster. *It is always amazing for me to see how the colour pigments of the earth change so dramatically within a day and a certain light situation. As if the clay walls had their own emotional world and could express it through their colour. Nature is truly the co-author in all this buildings.*

Dasselbe Prinzip des Schattenspiels findet sich im Kleinen angewandt, bei den intuitiv und partizipativ gestalteten Reliefs aus Lehmputz. Es ist für mich immer wieder erstaunlich zu sehen, wie sich die Farbpigmente der Erde innerhalb eines Tages und einer bestimmten Lichtsituation so dramatisch wandeln. Als ob die Lehmwände eine eigene Gefühlswelt hätten und diese über die Farbigkeit ausdrücken könnten. Die Natur ist wahrlich die Co-Autorin in all diesen Bauten.

As the locally available material is primarily clay, it is a simple matter of making the best of it. Restriction unleashes creativity. It is not only the visual result that is beautiful, but also the working process in which everyone can participate.
Da das lokal vorhandene Material primär Lehm ist, gilt es, einfach das Beste daraus zu machen. Einschränkung setzt Kreativität frei. Nicht nur das visuelle Ergebnis ist schön, auch der Arbeitsprozess, bei dem alle mitwirken können, ist es.

What fascinates me when travelling is the culturally different approach to light. *When I went to Bangladesh for the first time as a development apprentice in 1997/98, my fondest memories are connected with the power cuts in the evening. Or rather, the fact that many places had no electricity at all.*

In the evening, between six and half past six, the sun sets as a big red disk. Then the small kerosene lamps were lit and it was time to get together. If it was too hot in the huts, people gathered outside under the starry sky, talked and sang a lot. I learned quite a few Bengali folk songs there, in exchange for Bavarian ones. Often we gave each other a head massage while reviewing the day.

Light was precious, so it was shared. *The children huddled around a small lamp to do schoolwork. I learned so much on those evenings, not just a language and culture, but, more importantly, a clearer perspective on life.*

Since electricity is no longer a luxury, everything is lit in brightest white. It is certainly productive to be able to read and work after sunset. Light no longer has to be shared and more individual freedom is possible. But how much magic, how much contemplation, trusting closeness and tranquillity has been lost?

Was mich beim Reisen fasziniert, ist der kulturell unterschiedliche Umgang mit Licht. Als ich 1997/98 zum ersten Mal als Entwicklungslehrling nach Bangladesch ging, sind meine schönsten Erinnerungen mit den Stromausfällen am Abend verbunden. Oder viel mehr mit der Tatsache, dass viele Orte überhaupt keinen Stromanschluss hatten.

Am Abend, zwischen sechs und halb sieben geht die Sonne als grosse, rote Scheibe unter. Dann wurden die kleinen Kerosinlampen angezündet und es war Zeit, um zusammenzukommen. Wenn es in den Hütten zu heiss war, hat man sich draussen unter dem Sternenhimmel eingefunden, geredet und viel gesungen. Dort habe ich etliche bengalische Volkslieder gelernt, im Austausch zu bayerischen. Oft gab man sich gegenseitig eine Kopfmassage während man den Tag Revue passieren liess.

Licht war kostbar, daher wurde es geteilt. Die Kinder rückten um eine kleine Lampe zusammen, um Schularbeiten zu machen. An diesen Abenden habe ich so viel gelernt, nicht nur eine Sprache und Kultur, sondern vor allem eine klarere Sichtweise auf das Leben.

Seit Strom kein Luxus mehr ist, wird alles grell weiss ausgeleuchtet. Sicherlich ist es produktiv, wenn man nach Sonnenuntergang noch lesen und arbeiten kann. Licht muss auch nicht mehr geteilt werden und mehr individuelle Freiheit ist möglich. Aber wie viel Magie, Kontemplation und vertrauensvolle Nähe und Ruhe ist verloren gegangen?

95: Sharing the light. /// 95: Das Licht teilen.

96/97: Minoti, cooking rice for her family.
96/07: Minoti, die Reis für ihre Familie kocht.

What is the right amount of light?

Was ist das richtige Mass an Licht?

Weibliche Kraft

Female Strength

Embroidery of "Superwomen" on sari blanket.
Stickarbeiten an «Superfrauen» auf Sari-Decke.

Superwomen

Superfrauen

I am fortunate to collaborate with many wonderful women around the world. To get to the bottom of what "being female" can express, I asked the question: ***"What does 'woman' mean to you?"***

The answers can be watched on video through the QR codes.
Mittels QR-Codes kann man die Antworten auf Video sehen.

Zu meinem Glück darf ich mit vielen wundervollen Frauen überall auf der Welt zusammenarbeiten. Um auf die Spur zu kommen, was «weiblich sein» ausdrücken kann, habe ich die Frage gestellt: **«Was bedeutet ›Frau‹ für dich?»**

"Woman means mother. Mother is a storehouse of love."

Samya, 13 years, METI student, Bangladesh

«Frau bedeutet Mutter. Die Mutter ist ein Vorratshaus für Liebe.»

99–105: We asked the METI students to draw their personal superwoman – often it was their mother, sometimes their teacher or their aunt. In any case, all superwomen have something in common: they are super stylish! The drawings were transformed into embroideries by "Dipdii Textiles". (Project management: Klara Haug; Assistant: Lene Jünger)

99–105: Wir haben die METI-Schüler:innen gebeten, ihre persönliche Superfrau zu zeichnen – oft war es ihre Mutter, manchmal ihre Lehrerin oder ihre Tante. Auf jeden Fall haben alle Superfrauen etwas gemeinsam: Sie sind super stylisch! Die Zeichnungen wurden von «Dipdii Textiles» in Stickereien übertragen. (Projektmanagement: Klara Haug; Assistenz: Lene Jünger)

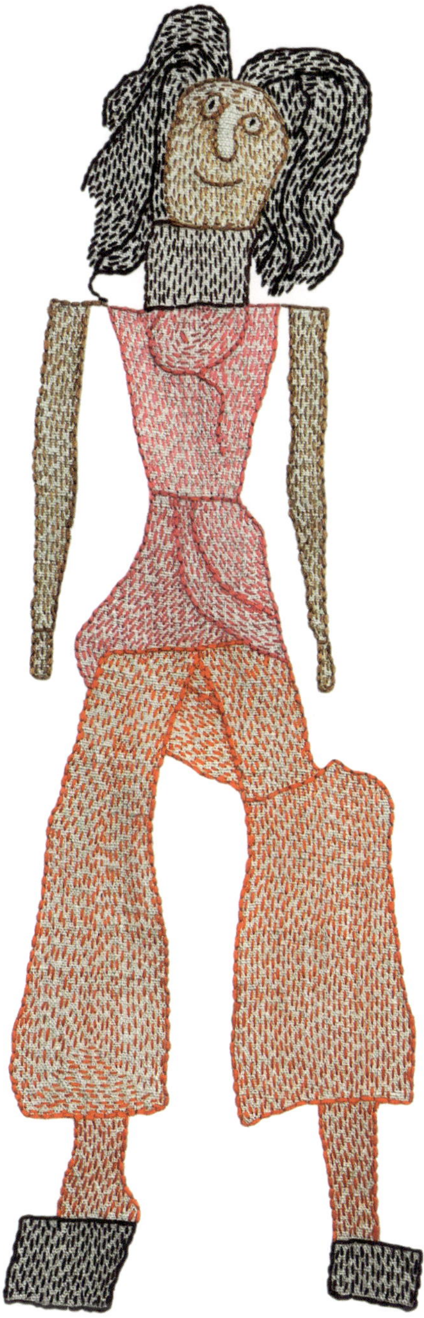

"A woman does not give up. When she falls, she rises."

Stella, 34 years, clay plastering master, Ghana

«Eine Frau gibt nicht auf. Wenn sie fällt, steht sie wieder auf.»

"Kind and caring!"

Mary, 29 years, and Mercy, 36 years, clay plastering masters, Ghana

«Freundlich und fürsorglich!»

"Woman means many responsibilities and patience."

Alika, 35 years, Dipdii Manager, Bangladesh

«Frau bedeutet viel Verantwortung und Geduld.»

"Compassionate and strong!"

Vumika, 28 years, Dipdii embroidery master, Bangladesh

«Mitfühlend und stark!»

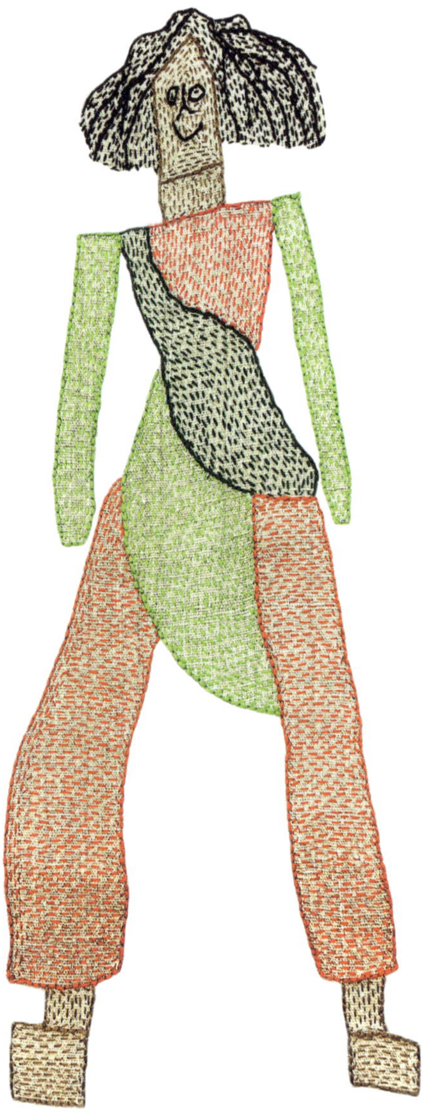

"Fierce and powerful!"

Maloti, 32 years, Dipdii embroidery master, Bangladesh

«Kämpferisch und mächtig!»

"Women will overcome all barriers with their confidence."

Himu, 14 years, METI student, Bangladesh

«Frauen werden durch ihre Zuversicht alle Hindernisse überwinden.»

"We can do anything."

Ronjona, 36 years, Dipdii embroidery master, Bangladesh

«Wir können alles schaffen.»

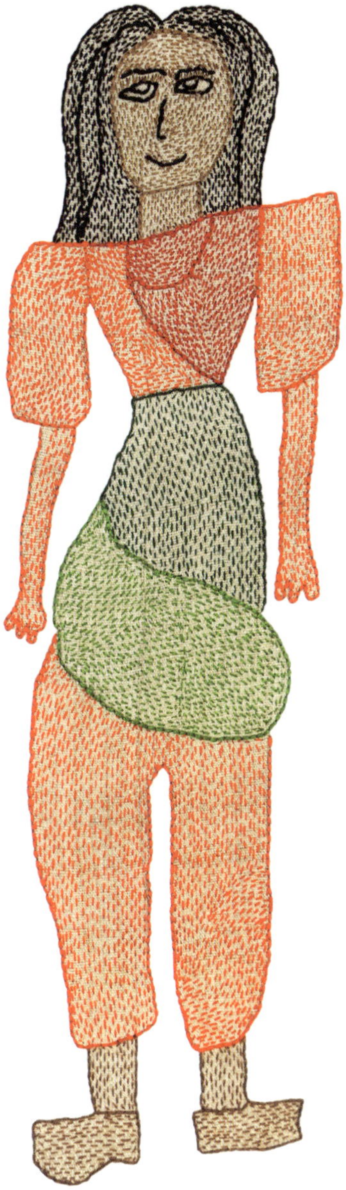

"Invaluable and mother!"

Molika, 31 years, Dipdii embroidery master, Bangladesh

«Unbezahlbar und eine Mutter!»

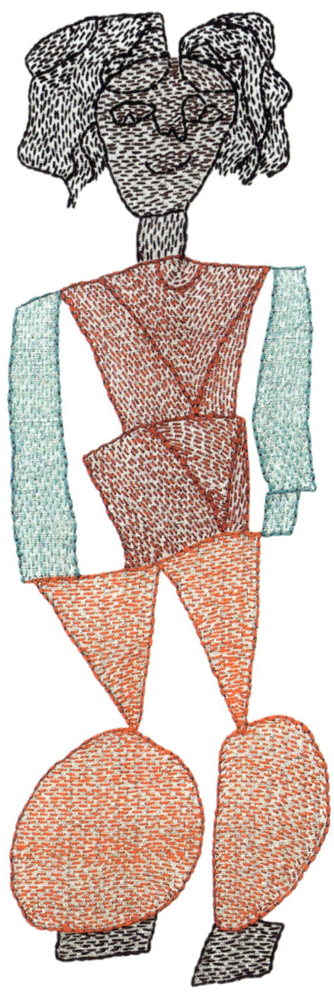

"Women have a special sense for beauty and the important things in life."

Ida, 9 years, and Angelika, 46 years, Austria

«Frauen haben einen speziellen Sinn für das Schöne und die wichtigen Dinge im Leben.»

"Intuition and beauty."

Elke, 57 years, fashion designer, Germany

«Intuition und Schönheit.»

"Healing. Powerful and loving."

Irmgard, 81 years, and Mirjam, 15 years, Germany

«Heilend. Stark und liebevoll.»

"Sensitivity and sisterhood."

Stefania, 29 years, architect, Italy/Brasil

«Einfühlungsvermögen und Schwesternschaft.»

"Superwomen", embroidery on sari blanket, 82 × 47 cm

«Superfrauen», Stickerei auf Sari-Decke, 82 × 47 cm

The Birth Space in Hittisau, Austria focuses on the theme of birth.
Der Gebärraum in Hittisau, Österreich stellt die Thematik Geburt in den Mittelpunkt.

One of my favourite design tasks was the development of a space for giving birth *in collaboration with Anka Dür, Martin Rauch and Sabrina Summer for the Women's Museum in Hittisau, Austria. It is almost unbelievable that we, as a society and architects' community, have not developed a contemporary typology for the greatest creative act of a human being – that of a woman!*

Giving birth cannot be reduced to a mere function. The birth of a new life is always a miracle. *And a major feat of strength. How can we best support the mother to open up? And how can the first moment as an independent being be designed as a fundamental trust-building experience for the child?*

Eine meiner schönsten Entwurfsaufgaben war die Entwicklung eines Gebärraumes gemeinsam mit Anka Dür, Martin Rauch und Sabrina Summer für das Frauenmuseum in Hittisau, Österreich. Fast nicht zu glauben, dass wir als Gesellschaft und Architektenzunft keine zeitgemässe Typologie für den grössten kreativen Akt eines Menschen – einer Frau – entwickelt haben!

Das Gebären lässt sich nicht nur auf die blosse Funktion reduzieren. Die Entstehung eines neuen Lebens ist immer auch ein Wunder. Und ein Kraftakt. Wie kann man die Mutter dabei bestmöglich unterstützen, sich zu öffnen? Wie lässt sich der erste Moment als eigenständiges Wesen für das Kind zu einer Urvertrauen stärkenden Erfahrung gestalten?

"Birth Space: floor plan", embroidery on sari blanket, 90 × 110 cm
«Gebärraum: Grundrissplan», Stickerei auf Sari-Decke, 90 × 110 cm

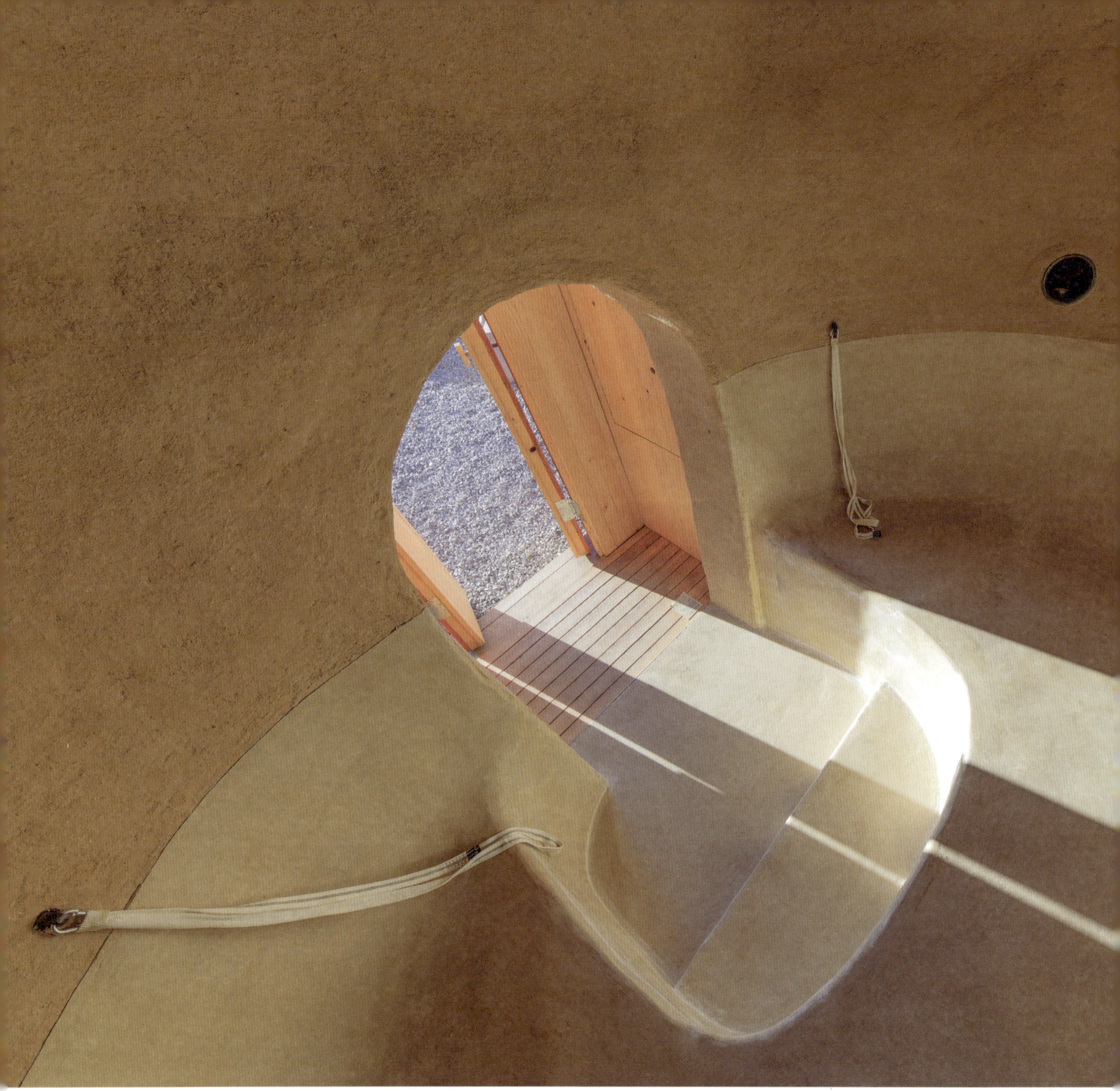

Interior of the birthing room, built of straw-clay bricks, protected from the outside with coloured wooden shingles and partly plastered with tadelakt on the inside. /// Innenraum des Gebärraumes, gebaut aus Stroh-Lehm-Ziegeln, von aussen geschützt mit farbigen Holzschindeln und im Inneren teils mit Tadelakt verputzt.

Earth, as a sensual material that conveys a feeling of comfort and has always been perceived as a creative, feminine element, forms an archaic birthing cave here: ***Mother Earth!***

Lehm – als sinnliches, Geborgenheit vermittelndes Material und als jeher als schöpferisches, weibliches Element wahrgenommen – formt hier eine archaische Geburtshöhle: **Mutter Erde!**

In 2016 and 2017, over a million Rohingya fled across the border from neighbouring Myanmar to Bangladesh in order to survive the genocide. *Since then, they have been stranded there in the Kutupalong camp, among others. I have twice been to the camp, which is one of the largest in the world.*

What moved me most was the situation of the women. *From the age of puberty, girls normally are only allowed to leave the tent to go to the public toilets. This means that the women spend their time in sweltering heat under plastic tarpaulins and have no opportunities to actively shape their lives. It is almost impossible for me to imagine how they can bear the inner pain of the atrocities they have experienced – from being raped to having to watch their husbands and children being murdered.*

Together with the NGO "OBAT Helpers", we asked the women to embroider their thoughts on textiles. *This is one of their messages to us: "We don't do anything for joy. We just pass the time sitting or sleeping. If we do attempt anything, especially in public spaces, we will face scrutiny." Embroidering enabled them to come together, at least for a short time, and earn some money.*

In den Jahren 2016 und 2017 flohen über eine Million Rohingya vom benachbarten Myanmar über die Grenze nach Bangladesch, um den Genozid zu überleben. Seitdem sind sie dort unter anderem im Lager Kutupalong gestrandet. Ich war zweimal in dem Lager, das zu den grössten der Welt zählt.

Was mich am meisten berührt hat, war die Situation der Frauen. Ab der Pubertät darf ein Mädchen das Zelt im Regelfall nur mehr verlassen, um die öffentlichen Toiletten aufzusuchen. Das heisst, die Frauen verbringen ihre Zeit in brütender Hitze unter Plastikplanen und haben keine Möglichkeiten, ihr Leben zu gestalten. Es ist für mich fast nicht vorstellbar, wie sie die inneren Schmerzen der erlebten Gräueltaten aushalten können – von Vergewaltigung bis zum Zusehen müssen, wie ihre Männer und Kinder ermordet wurden.

Gemeinsam mit der NGO «OBAT Helpers» haben wir die Frauen gebeten, ihre Gedanken auf Textilien zu sticken. Das ist eine ihrer Botschaften an uns: «Wir tun nichts, was uns Freude macht. Wir verbringen die Zeit mit Schlafen oder Herumsitzen. Wann immer wir versuchen, etwas im öffentlichen Raum zu unternehmen, erfahren wir nur Gängelungen.» Das Sticken ermöglichte ihnen zumindest für kurze Zeit zusammenzukommen und etwas Geld zu verdienen.

Rohingya women in Kutupalong camp in Bangladesh came together to make their voices heard – through embroidered messages to us. 2020, 202 × 153 cm /// Rohingya Frauen im Camp Kutupalong in Bangladesch kamen zusammen, um ihrer Stimme Gehör zu verschaffen – durch gestickte Botschaften an uns. 2020, 202 × 153 cm

"Dream house with helicopter and clouds", embroidered Rohingya child's drawing on sari blanket, 125 × 185 cm

«Traumhaus mit Helikopter und Wolken», gestickte Rohingya Kinderzeichnung auf Sari-Decke, 125 × 185 cm

When I was in the Kutupalong refugee camp with my student group from Harvard University, we asked the children to draw their dream houses for us. Most of them resemble the ones that were burned down in their home country. The mothers embroidered the drawings for us. How must they have felt when they captured the hopeful images of their children on the textiles? ***Migration has been around for as long as there have been people. Why haven't we developed better solutions yet?***

Als ich mit meiner Studentengruppe von der Harvard University im Flüchtlingslager Kutupalong war, baten wir die Kinder, für uns ihre Traumhäuser zu zeichnen. Meist ähneln sie denen, die in ihrer Heimat niedergebrannt wurden. Die Mütter haben die Zeichnungen für uns gestickt. Wie mögen sie sich dabei gefühlt haben, als sie die hoffnungsvollen Bilder ihrer Kinder auf den Textilien festhielten? **Migration gibt es solange es Menschen gibt. Warum haben wir noch keine besseren Lösungen entwickelt?**

Detail from the embroidered children's drawing with sun, helicopter, moon and star. 127 × 190 cm
Detail aus der gestickten Kinderzeichnung mit Sonne, Helikopter, Mond und Stern. 127 × 190 cm

The textiles were prepared by the "Dipdii Textiles" craftswomen in the north of the country, with fine embroidery patterns, as seen in the top left corner of the roof. The women in the refugee camp completed them. ***Visually, the embroideries are very different. One can feel the pain of the Rohingya women in each of the stitches.***

Die Zeichnungen wurden von den «Dipdii Textiles»-Handwerkerinnen im Norden des Landes vorbereitet, mit feinen Stickmustern, so wie im linken oberen Rand des Daches sichtbar. Die Frauen im Flüchtlingslager haben sie vervollständigt. **Optisch unterscheiden sich die Stickarten sehr deutlich. Man kann den Schmerz der Rohingya Frauen in jedem der Nadelstiche erahnen.**

Detail from the embroidery "Dream House with boy, mother and Bengali flag", based on a Rohingya child's drawing.
Ausschnitt aus der Stickerei «Traumhaus mit Jungem, Mutter und bengalischer Flagge», basierend auf der Zeichnung eines Rohingya Kindes.

"Dream house with boy, mother and Bengali flag", embroidered Rohingya child's drawing on sari blanket, 2021, 130 × 153 cm
«Traumhaus mit Jungem, Mutter und bengalischer Flagge», gestickte Rohingya Kinderzeichnung auf Sari-Decke, 2021, 130 × 153 cm

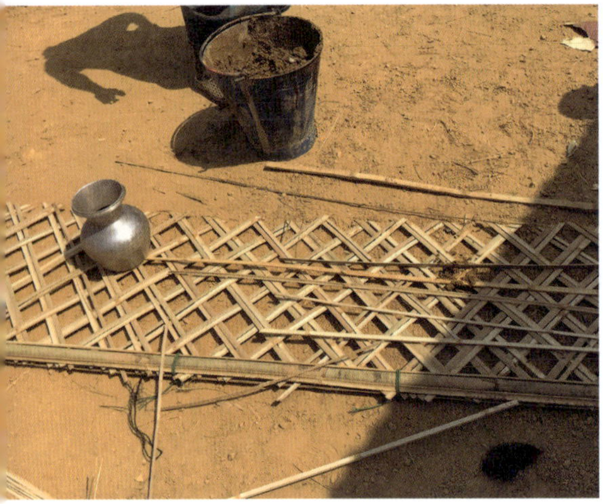

Workshop with "OBAT Helpers" in Kutupalong, currently the largest refugee camp in the world. Here are the first attempts to reinforce the woven bamboo walls with clay and make them fireproof.
Workshop mit «OBAT Helpers» in Kutupalong, dem derzeit grössten Flüchtlingslager der Welt. Hier die ersten Versuche, die Bambusflechtwände mit Lehm zu verstärken und feuerfest zu gestalten.

***Beautification is a woman's job – or so I thought.** Until I was taught otherwise in the Kutupalong refugee camp. I got together with some craftsmen to look for a way to make woven bamboo walls fireproof and more solid with clay plaster. We applied the clay together. I spontaneously started modelling an ornamental relief on it. It was time-consuming and I asked the men for help. "That's women's work, we don't do that," was their response. But at some point, because they either got bored of watching or it started itching in their fingers, they hesitantly started to work on the ornament. The more beautiful it became, the more they got into it. I had to get to my next appointment and left the building site. When I came back half an hour later, the men were still contemplatively – and almost tenderly – at work. Visibly happy.*

Verschönern ist Frauensache – so dachte ich. Bis ich im Flüchtlingslager Kutupalong eines Besseren belehrt wurde. Ich kam mit einigen Handwerkern zusammen, um nach einer Möglichkeit zu suchen, geflochtene Bambuswände mit Lehmputz feuerfest und solider zu gestalten. Wir brachten gemeinsam den Lehmputz auf. Spontan begann ich, darauf ein ornamentales Relief zu modellieren. Das war zeitaufwendig und ich bat die Männer um Unterstützung. «Das ist Frauenarbeit, das machen wir nicht», war ihre Antwort. Aber irgendwann wurde ihnen entweder das Zuschauen langweilig oder es juckte sie in den Fingern und sie begannen zögernd, am Ornament mitzuarbeiten. Je schöner es wurde, desto mehr wuchs der Eifer. Ich musste zu meinem nächsten Termin und verliess die Baustelle. Als ich nach einer halben Stunde noch einmal vorbeischaute, waren die Männer immer noch kontemplativ – und fast zärtlich – am Werkeln. Sichtlich glücklich.

I had a similar experience with my male colleagues in Ghana, who usually almost fight over who gets to use the big sledgehammer. Once the initial reluctance has been overcome, they usually really enjoy bringing their finer, softer aspects to the surface. ***Giving space to the feminine in us feels good, and not just for women!***

The clay plaster is embellished with ornaments. Hesitantly at first, then with growing pleasure.
Der Lehmputz wird mit Ornamenten verschönert. Erst zögerlich, dann mit wachsender Freude.

Ähnliches erlebte ich bei meinen männlichen Mitarbeitern in Ghana, die sich sonst im Allgemeinen fast darum prügeln, wer den grossen Schlaghammer benutzen darf. Nachdem die erste Scheu überwunden ist, geniessen sie es regelrecht, ihre feineren und weicheren Seiten an die Oberfläche zu lassen. **Dem Weiblichen in uns Raum zu geben, tut nicht nur Frauen gut!**

Detail on the wall of Nichodemus House at the Don Bosco Earth Campus in Ghana. Wipe your clay-encrusted hands on your pants and document the day's work. Time to rest.
Wanddetail am Nichodemus House im Don Bosco Earth Campus in Ghana. Die Lehm verkrusteten Hände an der Hose abwischen und das Tageswerk dokumentieren. Feierabend.

Growing Light

At the risk of making myself vulnerable, I nevertheless dare to take a look at my dark sides that need light. All the cracks and burn marks that I don't like to pay attention to, even though they affect me and inhibit my zest of life. Sometimes it's anger and probably also a little envy that hits me when I see how some colleagues make it easy for themselves with strategies that I would regard as greenwashing.

The main thing that nags at me is my impatience that the positive development is not progressing as quickly as I would like. Sometimes, it makes me almost implode. And the annoying doubts that sometimes keep me from being fully in my power, those self-doubts paired with the self-imposed pressure of expectations to do everything perfectly. I feel that many people experience this pressure these days.

Wachsendes Licht

Auf die Gefahr hin, mich angreifbar zu machen, wage ich trotzdem einen Blick auf meine dunklen Seiten, die Licht brauchen. All die Risse und Brandflecken, denen ich nicht so gerne meine Aufmerksamkeit schenke, obwohl sie mich beeinflussen und in meiner Lebensfülle hemmen. Manchmal ist es der Ärger und wohl auch etwas Neid, der mich dann trifft, wenn ich sehe, wie es sich manche Kollegen mit Strategien leicht machen, die ich als Greenwashing betrachte.

Schwer zwickt mich vor allem die Ungeduld, dass die positive Entwicklung nicht so schnell vorangeht, wie ich es gerne hätte. Die lässt mich manchmal schier implodieren. Und die nervigen Zweifel, die manchmal davon abhalten, voll in meiner Kraft zu sein, diese Selbstzweifel gepaart mit selbst auferlegtem Erwartungsdruck, alles perfekt machen zu wollen. Ich glaube, diesen Druck spüren heutzutage viele.

There is fear behind doubting and striving for perfection. *The fear of not being enough. Having to show our best side in order to be loved ... That's not necessary. With all the scratches, wrinkles, cracks and patches on top, we are worth it!*

How can we mend these tears in the fabric of life so that they become – not perfect – but harmonious, beautiful? *How about: Stop judging and criticising others and ourselves? Turn this inner critic, who is constantly putting his two cents in, into a friend. Expand our own perspectives with empathy. And above all: let love grow.* ***Love makes everything lighter.***

Change is difficult? Yes and no. Actually, one thought is enough. Like a little spark. All changes come about in the smallest of things, even the creation of our universe. It wasn't a big bang. It was a miniscule, infinitely powerful light that contained the entire energy of all creation. *The indescribable, universal spark of light that shaped everything is also within us. This light naturally wants to expand, undiminished by fears and doubts.*

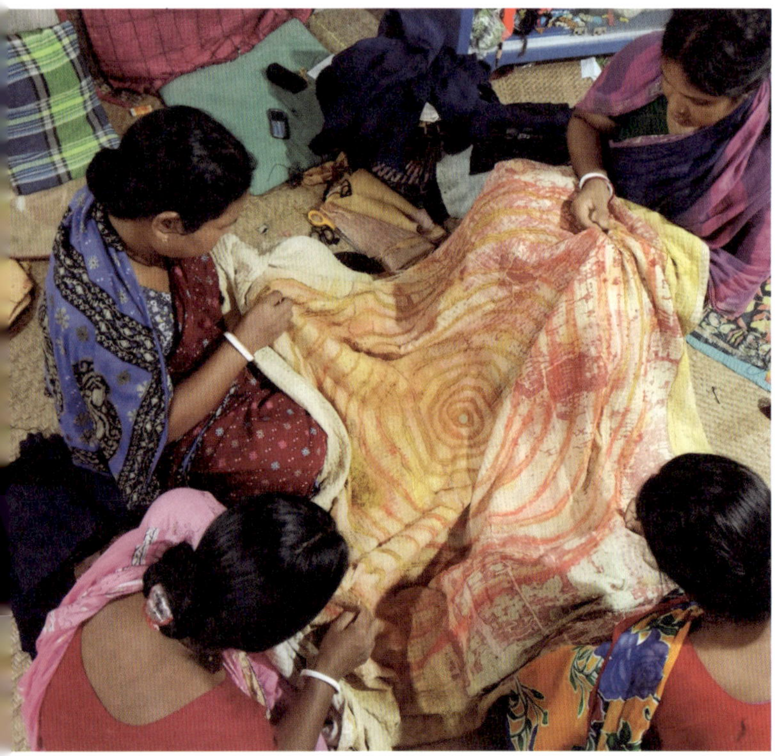

Embroidery work on "Solar Spiral" in Rudrapur.
Stickarbeiten an «Sonnenspirale» in Rudrapur.
121: Detail "Solar Spiral" /// 121: Detail «Sonnenspirale»

Es steckt Angst hinter dem Zweifeln und Streben nach Perfektion. Die Angst, nicht genug zu sein. Uns von unserer besten Seite zeigen zu müssen, um geliebt zu werden ... Dabei ist das gar nicht nötig. Mit allen Kratzern, Falten, Rissen, Flicken obendrauf, sind wir es wert!

Wie kann man diese Risse im Lebensgewebe flicken, auf dass sie – nicht perfekt – aber harmonisch, schön werden? Wie wäre es mit: Aufhören zu werten, zu kritisieren, die anderen und uns selber? Diesen inneren Kritiker, der ständig seinen Senf abgibt, in einen Freund, eine Freundin verwandeln. Den Blickwinkel emphatisch erweitern. Und vor allem: **die Liebe wachsen lassen. Durch diese wird alles lichter.**

Veränderung ist schwierig? Ja und nein. Tatsächlich genügt ein Gedanke. Wie ein kleiner Funken. Alle Veränderungen entstehen im kleinen, sogar die Entstehung unseres Universums. Das war kein lauter Knall. Es war ein winzig kleines, unendlich starkes Licht, dem die gesamte Schöpfungsenergie innewohnte. Der unbeschreibliche, universale Lichtfunke, der alles gestaltet hat, ist auch in uns. Dieses Licht will sich naturgemäss ausweiten, ungemindert von Ängsten und Zweifeln.

"Solar Spiral", 2025, embroidery on sari blanket, 170 × 214 cm
«Sonnenspirale», 2025, Stickerei auf Sari-Decke, 170 × 214 cm

Light is a force of nature.
We humans are a force of nature too.
Especially when we stand together.

Licht ist eine natürliche Kraft.
Auch wir Menschen sind eine natürliche Kraft.
Ganz besonders, wenn wir zusammenhalten.

Acknowledgments

My heartfelt thanks goes to Angelika Mathis for her sensitive, intuitive and absolutely beautiful graphic design of this book. And above all for being such a great partner throughout the entire process of this project. A very special thanks goes to Isabel Zumtobel for her great support beyond the book and the accompanying exhibition, for the women in Bangladesh. Thanks to the team at Zumtobel Group for their multifaceted commitment – from the organisation and management, above all Agata Spatzek and Natalie Kreutzer, to the practical support of Dietmar Egender – to the upgrading of our lighting situation in our textile workshop in Bangladesh with Zumtobel Group luminaires and professional lighting design by Kay-Uwe Dingeldein and Davide Siciliano.
Thank you Lars Müller – what a pleasure to finally work with you – after you were my teacher for book design at the GSD many years ago …!
Thanks to all the great photographers, who enchant these pages with their atmospheric images and for donating their photographs. And especially to Kurt Hörbst, who has been sharing his talents with me since my first project, the METI School 20 years ago!

This book would not have been possible without the wonderful embroidery masters at "Dipdii Textiles": Alika Khatun, Mallika Debsarma, Binodini Debsarma, Chabita Rani Roy, Anjuara Begum, Nitika Rani Roy, Maloti Rani, Ranzana Roy, Mukta Rani Roy, Swapana Debsarma, Swapana Rani Debi, Parthona Rani Debsarma, Bhumika Rani Debsarma, Razia Akter, Maloti Soren, Razina Akter, Dipali Rani and Aklima Akter – "onek dhannabad!" You know how much I love you …
Elke Burmeister-Haug and Klara Haug for such appreciative and humorous guidance of the embroidery work in Bangladesh. Special thanks to the Anandaloy and METI kids for their beautiful drawings.
My biggest respect and admiration to the great artisans in Ghana, especially Baninya Yaa, Kojokumah Ngaabe, Najumbu Adwoa, Kwame Ntiyasu Afia and Kojo Nboogma, for their wonderful work and for everything you teach me. Thank you Dipshikha, Prem Shankar und Sathya Narayanan for your continuous support! And all my project partners, especially Lord Zigato and Martin Rauch.

Last but not least, a big, big thank you to my fantastic team, who has been with me through thick and thin, and to my favorite team of all times: my family!

Danksagung

Mein tief empfundener Dank geht an Angelika Mathis für ihre sensible, intuitive und absolut schöne grafische Gestaltung dieses Buches. Und vor allem dafür, dass sie mir eine so grossartige Partnerin im gesamten Prozess dieses Projekts war. Ein ganz besonderer Dank geht an Isabel Zumtobel für ihre grossartige Unterstützung über das Buch und die begleitende Ausstellung hinaus, für die Frauen in Bangladesch. Danke an das Zumtobel Group Team für das vielfältige Engagement – von der Organisation und dem Projektmanagement, allen voran Agata Spatzek und Natalie Kreutzer, über die praktische Unterstützung von Dietmar Egender – bis zur Aufwertung unserer Lichtsituation in unserer Textilwerkstatt in Bangladesch mit Zumtobel Group Leuchten und professioneller Lichtplanung durch Kay-Uwe Dingeldein und Davide Siciliano.
Danke Lars Müller – was für ein Vergnügen, endlich mit dir zu arbeiten – nachdem du vor vielen Jahren mein Lehrer für Buchgestaltung an der GSD warst …!
Danke an all die grossartigen Fotografen, die diese Seiten mit ihren stimmungsvollen Aufnahmen verzaubern und ihre Fotografien noch dazu gespendet haben. Und ganz besonders an Kurt Hörbst, der seit meinem ersten Projekt seine Talente mit mir teilt, der METI-Schule vor 20 Jahren!

Ohne die wunderbaren Stickerinnen von «Dipdii Textiles» wäre dieses Buch nicht möglich gewesen: Alika Khatun, Mallika Debsarma, Binodini Debsarma, Chabita Rani Roy, Anjuara Begum, Nitika Rani Roy, Maloti Rani, Ranzana Roy, Mukta Rani Roy, Swapana Debsarma, Swapana Rani Debi, Parthona Rani Debsarma, Bhumika Rani Debsarma, Razia Akter, Maloti Soren, Razina Akter, Dipali Rani und Aklima Akter – «onek dhannabad!» Ihr wisst, wie gern ich euch habe …
Elke Burmeister-Haug und Klara Haug für so wertschätzende und humorvolle Anleitungen der Stickarbeiten in Bangladesch. Besonderer Dank an die Anandaloy- und METI-Kids für ihre wunderschönen Zeichnungen.
Mein grösster Respekt und meine Bewunderung für die grossartigen Handwerker:innen in Ghana, insbesondere Baninya Yaa, Kojokumah Ngaabe, Najumbu Adwoa, Kwame Ntiyasu Afia und Kojo Nboogma, für ihre wunderbare Arbeit und für alles, was ihr mir beibringt. Danke auch an Dipshikha, Prem Shankar und Sathya Narayanan für all ihre Unterstützung. Und all meinen Projektpartnern, ganz besonders Lord Zigato und Martin Rauch.

Zu guter Letzt ein ganz grosses Dankeschön an mein fantastisches Team, das mit mir durch dick und dünn geht, und an mein Lieblingsteam: meine Familie!

Embroidery masters of "Dipdii Textiles", Bangladesh
Stickmeisterinnen von «Dipdii Textiles», Bangladesch

Tatale plastering gang, Ghana
Tatale Verputzerinnen-Truppe, Ghana

"Dipdii Textiles" is grateful for every donation:
«Dipdii Textiles» ist dankbar für jede Spende:
Verein zur Förderung der textilen Handwerkskunst e.V.,
IBAN: DE37 7105 0000 0020 7381 83, BIC: BYLADEM1BGL

Architecture credits /// Architekturnachweise

***Anandaloy,* Centre for People with Disabilities and "Dipdii Textiles" Workshop, Rudrapur, Bangladesh, 2017** (pp. 7, 26–27, 36–39, 74–75)
Architecture /// Architektur: Studio Anna Heringer
Project management /// Projektmanagement: Stefano Mori

***Pepita,* Biennale Venice, Italy, 2016** (p. 63)
This sculpture was part of the installation "Earth Works", Heringer & Rauch in collaboration with Andres Lepik. /// Diese Skulptur war Teil der Installation «Earth Works», Heringer & Rauch in Zusammenarbeit mit Andres Lepik.
Architecture /// Architektur: Anna Heringer & Martin Rauch
Project management /// Projektmanagement: Stefano Mori

***OMICRON Monolith and Zeppelin,* Klaus, Austria, 2015** (pp. 64–67)
Concept and design /// Konzept und Design: Anna Heringer & Martin Rauch
Project realisation /// Projektrealisierung: Lehm Ton Erde Baukunst GmbH

***METI School,* Rudrapur, Bangladesh, 2006** (pp. 68–73, 77, 80–81)
Architecture /// Architektur: Anna Heringer (Design), Eike Roswag-Klinge (Technical Planning)

***DESI Vocational School for Electrical Training,* Rudrapur, Bangladesh, 2008** (pp. 78–79)
Architecture /// Architektur: Studio Anna Heringer
Site supervision /// Bauleitung: Montu Ram Shaw, Stefan Neumann

***Don Bosco Earth Campus,* Tatale, Ghana, since 2019** (ongoing) (front cover, front endpaper, pp. 82–93, 118, 124–125)
Architecture /// Architektur: Studio Anna Heringer with Lord Zigato
Design /// Gestaltung: Anna Heringer
Project team /// Projektteam: Katharina Lehmann, Florian Wick, Alice Guilhou, Viktoriya Nikolova, Rebecca Temperanza, Stefania Bellato, Ania Chorzepa, Sophie Scheurer
Engineering and site management /// Bautechnik und Bauleitung: Lord Zigato, Christian Paul Agboada and foreman Sampson Dousa

***Birth Space,* Frauenmuseum Hittisau, Austria, 2020** (pp. 106–109)
Architecture /// Architektur: Anka Dür, Anna Heringer, Martin Rauch, Sabrina Summer **In collaboration with ///** In Zusammenarbeit mit: Brigitta Soraperra, Stefania Pitscheider Soraperra

Anna Heringer

For Anna Heringer, architecture is a tool to improve lives. She became internationally known in 2006 with the construction of the METI School in Rudrapur, Bangladesh, which she designed as her diploma thesis at the University of Art and Design Linz. Since then, Heringer has further developed and disseminated her award-winning architectural approach through buildings in Asia, Africa and Europe as well as through teaching architecture at the University of Liechtenstein, Harvard University and ETH Zurich, among others. Her central concern is to use architecture as a catalyst for local development, particularly through the use of natural building materials such as earth, bamboo and wood and the participation of users in the construction process.

Her work has been exhibited worldwide, including the MoMA New York, the Cité de l'architecture & du patrimoine Paris, the Museo ICO Madrid, the V&A Museum London and the Venice Biennale. She has received numerous awards for her work, including the Aga Khan Award for Architecture, the Global Award for Sustainable Architecture, the New European Bauhaus Prize, the Philippe Rotthier European Prize for Architecture, the OBEL Award and the Max Beckmann Prize. UNESCO awarded her an honorary professorship for "Earthen Architecture, Building Cultures and Sustainable Development". In 2022, she was honoured with the Order of Merit by Germany's Federal President Frank-Walter Steinmeier.

Besides being an architect, activist and educator, she is the CEO of "Dipdii Textiles", a women's collaboration for fair fashion and textile art, an author and a mother. Her motto in design practice and life is simply "Form Follows Love".

Anna Heringer

Für Anna Heringer ist Architektur ein Werkzeug, um Lebensbedingungen zu verbessern. Internationale Bekanntheit erlangte sie 2006 mit dem Bau der METI-Schule in Bangladesch, die sie als Diplomarbeit an der Kunstuniversität Linz entwarf. Seitdem hat Heringer durch Bauten in Asien, Afrika und Europa sowie durch die Architekturlehre, unter anderem an der Universität Liechtenstein, der Harvard University und der ETH Zürich, ihren mehrfach ausgezeichneten Architekturansatz weiterentwickelt und verbreitet. Ihr zentrales Anliegen ist dabei, Architektur als Katalysator für lokale Entwicklung einzusetzen, insbesondere durch die Verwendung natürlicher Baumaterialien wie Lehm, Bambus und Holz und die Einbeziehung der Nutzer:innen im Bauprozess.

Ihre Arbeiten wurden in zahlreichen Museen weltweit ausgestellt, darunter im MoMA New York, in der Cité de l'architecture & du patrimoine Paris, im Museo ICO Madrid, im V&A Museum London und auf der Biennale in Venedig. Für ihre Arbeit erhielt sie unter anderem den Aga Khan Award for Architecture, den Global Award for Sustainable Architecture, den New European Bauhaus Preis, den Philippe Rotthier European Prize for Architecture, den OBEL Award und den Max-Beckmann-Preis. Die UNESCO verlieh ihr einen Ehrenprofessortitel für «Earthen Architecture, Building Cultures and Sustainable Development». 2022 wurde sie vom Bundespräsidenten Frank-Walter Steinmeier mit dem Bundesverdienstkreuz ausgezeichnet.

Neben ihren Tätigkeiten als Architektin, Aktivistin und Lehrende ist Anna Heringer auch CEO von «Dipdii Textiles», einer Frauenkooperative für faire Mode und Textilkunst, sowie Autorin und Mutter. Ihr Motto im kreativen Schaffen wie im Leben ist: «Form Follows Love».

The making of this book, Anna Heringer and Angelika Mathis
Entstehung dieses Buches, Anna Heringer und Angelika Mathis

Imprint /// Impressum

The Zumtobel Group aims to create well-being and improve people's quality of life through light – as a group, and through all its individual brands, Thorn, Tridonic and Zumtobel. As a leading supplier of innovative lighting solutions, the Group offers its customers around the world a comprehensive portfolio, where the focus is invariably on people and their needs. The company's know-how about the effects of light on people, acquired over decades, forms the basis for future-oriented lighting solutions that are increasingly energy- and resource-efficient while providing the best possible quality of light. The Group is based in Dornbirn in the Vorarlberg region of Austria.
The publication "LIGHT – the Natural Force that Makes Things Visible" was initiated by the Zumtobel Group for the design of its Artistic Annual Report 2024/25.

Die Zumtobel Group hat das Ziel, mit Licht Wohlbefinden zu schaffen und die Lebensqualität der Menschen zu verbessern – als Unternehmensgruppe und mit ihren Marken Thorn, Tridonic und Zumtobel. Als führender Anbieter innovativer Lichtlösungen bietet die Gruppe ihren Kunden weltweit ein umfassendes Portfolio, bei dem der Mensch und seine Bedürfnisse stets im Mittelpunkt stehen. Das über Jahrzehnte erworbene Know-how des Unternehmens über die Wirkung von Licht auf den Menschen bildet die Grundlage für zukunftsweisende Lichtlösungen, die immer noch energie- und ressourceneffizienter sind und gleichzeitig die bestmögliche Lichtqualität bieten. Der Sitz der Gruppe befindet sich in Dornbirn im österreichischen Vorarlberg.
Die Publikation «LICHT – die natürliche Kraft, die Dinge sichtbar macht» wurde von der Zumtobel Group im Zuge der Gestaltung ihres Artistic Annual Report 2024/25 initiiert.

Image Credits /// Bildnachweise

© Alika Kathun: p. 120
© Angelika Mathis: front endpaper back side, pp. 41, 42/43, 48, 107, 114, 121, back endpaper
© Anna Heringer: front cover, front endpaper, pp. 76, 82/83, 84/85, 86/87, 90, 93, 118, 125
© Bruno Klompfar: p. 63
© Cornelia Faisst: p. 92
© Dipshikha: p. 124 (middle)
© Don Bosco Tatale: p. 124 (right)
© Elke Burmeister: p. 124 (left)
© Fabio Marcato: pp. 14 (right), 15, 16/17, 18/19, 23, 99
© Günter König: pp. 20/21, 28/29, 30/31, 44/45, 47, 51, 52/53, 56/57, 60/61, 112/113, 122, back cover
© Iwan Baan: p. 7
© Klara Haug: p. 33
© Kurt Hörbst: pp. 14 (left), 26/27, 36/37, 38/39, 70/71, 73 (right), 74/75, 77, 80/81, 95, 96/97
© Laurenz Feinig: pp. 106, 108/109
© Museo ICO / César González: pp. 54/55, 58/59
© Naquib Hossain: pp. 78/79
© Nina Bröll: p. 126
© PMK / Rolf Bauerndick: pp. 72/73 (left)
© Shafiqur Rahman: pp. 116/117
© Shaowen Zhang and Tommy Scharperkotter: p. 111
© Studio Anna Heringer / Florian Wick: pp. 9, 13, 22, 32, 34/35, 100/101, 102/103, 104/105, 115
© Studio Anna Heringer / Katharina Lehmann: pp. 88/89
© Studio Anna Heringer / Stefano Mori: pp. 4, 25, 64/65, 66/67
© The Aga Khan Award for Architecture / B.K.S. Inan: pp. 68/69

Initiator /// Initiator — Zumtobel Group AG, Austria
Publisher /// Verlag — Lars Müller Publishers
Special thanks to /// Besonderer Dank an — Isabel Zumtobel
Author /// Autorin — Anna Heringer (www.anna-heringer.com)
Graphic design /// Gestaltung — Angelika Mathis (www.amgestalten.com)
Editor /// Redakteurin — Natalie Kreutzer (Zumtobel Group)
Project management /// Projektmanagement — Angelika Mathis (www.amgestalten.com), Agata Spatzek (Zumtobel Group)
Proofreading /// Korrektorat — Christine Fitz, Austria; Barbara Wrathall-Pohl, Austria
Lithography /// Lithografie — Günter König (fotokoenig.at)
Printing and binding /// Druck und Bindung — Druckerei Thurnher, Austria; Buchbinderei Kunesch, Austria
Paper /// Papier — Munken Lynx Rough; Wibalin Express Natural White

Zumtobel Group AG
Höchsterstrasse 8
6850 Dornbirn, Austria
T +43 5572 509-0
info@zumtobelgroup.com
www.z.lighting

Studio Anna Heringer
Rottmayrstrasse 24
83410 Laufen, Germany
T +49 8682 809781
office@anna-heringer.com
www.anna-heringer.com

Lars Müller Publishers
Pfingstweidstrasse 6
8005 Zurich, Switzerland
T +41 44 274 37 40
info@lars-muller.ch
www.lars-mueller-publishers.com

Lars Müller Publishers is supported by the Swiss Federal Office of Culture with a structural contribution for the years 2021–2025. /// Der Verlag Lars Müller Publishers wird vom Schweizer Bundesamt für Kultur mit einem Strukturbeitrag für die Jahre 2021–2025 unterstützt.

Product safety /// Produktsicherheit
Producer /// Hersteller: Lars Müller Publishers GmbH
Responsible person in accordance with EU Regulation 2023/988 (GPSR) /// Verantwortliche Person gemäss EU-Verordnung 2023/988 (GPSR): Michael Klein, sales representative / Verlagsvertretung, Hub 1, DE-84149 Velden, T +49 8742 964 552 2, gpsr@lars-muller.ch

ISBN 978-3-03778-797-7

Distributed in North America, Latin America and the Caribbean by ARTBOOK | D.A.P., www.artbook.com

Printed in Austria